A comprehensive

MATHEMATICS DICTIONARY
FOR GRADES K-8

including terms from the CCSS

M.W. PENN and **MONICA MERRITT**

Written by M. W. Penn and Monica Merritt
Design by Daphne Firos

————————————

Content © 2014 MathWord Press
Cover design © 2014 Daphne Firos

ISBN: 978-1-939431-07-3
Library of Congress Control Number: 2014935532

*A Comprehensive Mathematics Dictionary for Grades K-8
including terms used in the Common Core State Standards*
is published by MathWord Press.

————————————

MW Penn dedicates this work to her dear friend
Kumpati 'Bob' Narendra, Harold W. Cheel Professor
of Electrical Engineering at Yale University.

"Better than a thousand days of diligent study is one day with a great teacher." Japanese Proverb

---

Monica Merritt dedicates this work to her favorite young mathematicians, her daughters, Jasmine and Morgan.

ABACUS

A frame with wires or rods of beads that are moved to count or perform arithmetic computations. An ancient device, the abacus is still used in parts of the world, especially in the Far East. It can be used in the study of place value.

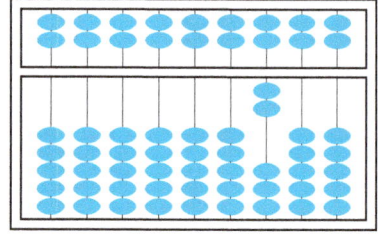

ABSCISSA

Another name for the x coordinate in Cartesian coordinate system.

(See CARTESIAN COORDINATE SYSTEM, X AXIS)

ABSOLUTE VALUE

The distance a number is from zero on the number line. Because absolute value gives a distance from 0, it is always a positive number.

Example: The absolute value of -3 , written | 3 |, is 3 because -3 is 3 units away from 0 on the number line.

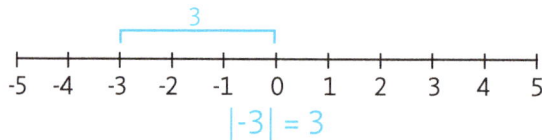

$|-3| = 3$

ABUNDANT NUMBER

A number that has proper divisors that, when added together, have a sum greater than that number.

Example: The proper divisors of 12 are 1, 2, 3, 4, and 6.
Sum of these divisors = 1 + 2 + 3 + 4 + 6 = 16.

ACCELERATION

Increasing the rate of velocity of an object; moving faster and faster in a specified direction.

When an object moves, it changes position. Velocity is a measure of the rate at which the object changes position and also of the direction of the motion. Therefore velocity is a vector quantity requiring both speed and direction.

Acceleration is also a vector quantity. It measures the rate at which an object increases its velocity. An object is accelerating if it is increasing its velocity.

Example: When a car begins to move, it starts from a standing position of no forward motion and then accelerates until it reaches the velocity which the driver wants to maintain. Once it reaches this velocity, it will stop accelerating and maintain its velocity.

(See SPEED, VECTOR, VELOCITY)

ACRE

A standard unit for measuring area in the customary system of measurement. An acre is equal to 43,560 square feet. It is used to measure land; one acre is a bit smaller than a football field. The unit, acre, originated as the amount of land one man and one pair of oxen could reasonably plow in one day.

ACUTE ANGLE

An angle that measures less than 90°. A 90° angle is called a right angle; right angles are the angles you see in the corners of a square or a rectangle.

Angles BAC and EDF are two examples of acute angles.

(See ANGLE, OBLIQUE, OBTUSE)

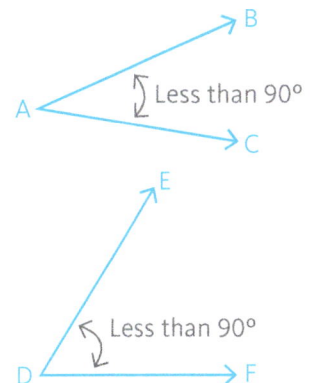

B

Less than 90°

A

C

E

Less than 90°

D   F

ACCURACY

Describes how close a given value is to the actual value in a measurement or a calculation.

Example: When the marks on a ruler are made closer together we can use the ruler to measure an object with more accuracy.

(See PRECISION)

ACUTE TRIANGLE

A triangle that contains three acute angles; a triangle with all internal angles measuring less than 90°.

These are examples of acute triangles.

(See TRIANGLE, INTERNAL ANGLE)

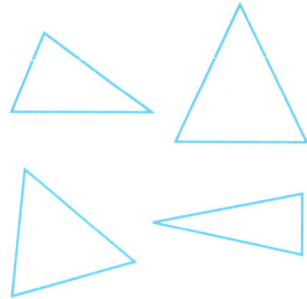

ADD

To find the sum of two or more numbers; to find the number of members of a set that is composed of the combined members of two or more sets. When we add, we bring two or more quantities together to make a new total.

For example, if one set contains 3 members and another contains 5, the combined set will contain 8 members. In mathematics notation we write this as an equation: $3 + 5 = 8$

OOO + OOOOO
=
OOOOOOOO

(See ADDITION, EQUATION)

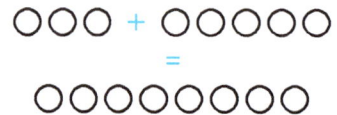

ADDEND

A number that we add to another number, or to more than one other number, to find the sum.

Example: In the computation: 4 + 5 = 9
4 and 5 are both addends.

ADDITION TABLE

A table that displays addition facts, or the sums of common addition operations.

The basic facts of addition are the 100 sums that result from adding all combinations of the 10 digits. This common addition table, used in elementary grades, provides a visual display of all of the combinations for the 10 digits.

Addition table of the basic addition facts for the ten digits of the base ten number system.

+	0	1	2	3	4	5	6	7	8	9
0	0	1	2	3	4	5	6	7	8	9
1	1	2	3	4	5	6	7	8	9	10
2	2	3	4	5	6	7	8	9	10	11
3	3	4	5	6	7	8	9	10	11	12
4	4	5	6	7	8	9	10	11	12	13
5	5	6	7	8	9	10	11	12	13	14
6	6	7	8	9	10	11	12	13	14	15
7	7	8	9	10	11	12	13	14	15	16
8	8	9	10	11	12	13	14	15	16	17
9	9	10	11	12	13	14	15	16	17	18

(See TABLE)

ADDITIVE INVERSE

Two numbers are additive inverses if their sum is zero. Additive inverses are the same distance from zero on the number line, but in opposite directions. The additive inverse of any number is the opposite of that number.

The additive inverse of a number n is -n.

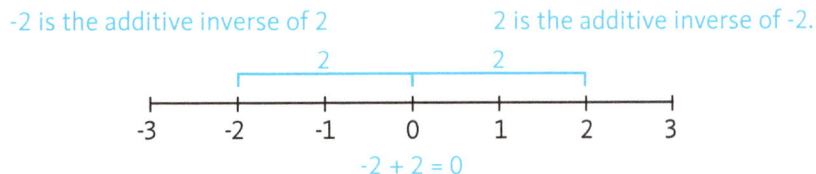

-2 is the additive inverse of 2   2 is the additive inverse of -2.

$$-2 + 2 = 0$$

ADJACENT

Lying next to each other. In mathematics, adjacent defines angles
or sides of polygons.

In plane geometry, adjacent angles have a common vertex and a common side
and do not overlap.

Adjacent sides of a polygon share a common vertex.

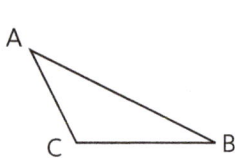

CAB and ABC
are adjacent angles

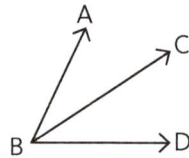

ABC and CBD
are adjacent angles

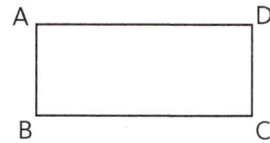

Line segments $\overline{AB}$ and $\overline{BC}$ are
adjacent sides of this rectangle

ALGEBRA

The study of operations on numbers using symbols for variables.

Algebra expands arithmetic operations by using symbols, often letters, to define
variables, which are numbers with values that are unknown or that will change.

Example of using a letter to denote an unknown quantity in a problem:
$10X \div 2 = 25$

This is an example of an algebraic equation, read 10 multiplied by some number,
X, and then divided by 2 equals 25. In this equation X is equal to 5.

Because algebra allows us to use symbols to represent any of a certain set of
numbers (such as, for example, any number in the set of all real numbers), it
allows us to describe laws that will hold for every number in the set. In this way,
algebra allows us to generalize specific arithmetic relationships and allows us to
explore patterns.

Examples of using a letter to generalize a relationship or fact:
The arithmetic fact that $5 + 5 = 5 \times 2$ or $2(5)$
and the fact that $6 + 6 = 6 \times 2$ or $2(6)$
are both cases of the algebraic statement $x + x = 2x$.
The fact that $3^2 = 3 \times 3$ and the fact that $6^2 = 6 \times 6$ can be stated as $Y^2 = Y \times Y$.

ALGEBRAIC EXPRESSION

An expression that contains one or more numbers, one or more variables, and one or more arithmetic operations.

Examples of an algebraic expression: $7x + 2$; $x^3 + 2x^2 - 8x$; $a + b^3$

ALGORITHM

A precisely defined procedure giving a step by step sequence of instructions used to complete a task. For example, algorithms detail how to solve a particular problem, compute, measure or estimate.

A defined procedure for a computation that gives the correct result in every case is a computational algorithm.

Example: A conventional algorithm that has been taught in public schools for decades is the 'standard addition' algorithm. It is the model in which tens are 'carried' from the 'ones' column to the 'tens' column, hundreds are 'carried' from the 'tens' column to the 'hundreds' column, etc.

$$\begin{array}{r} {\scriptstyle 2\ 1} \\ 462 \\ 88 \\ +\ 287 \\ \hline 837 \end{array}$$

(*See* COMPUTATION ALGORITHM)

ALTERNATE EXTERIOR ANGLES

When two straight lines are cut by a third line called a transversal, the pairs of angles formed outside the two lines and on the opposite sides of the transversal are called Alternate Exterior Angles.

Note: If two parallel lines are cut by a transversal, the alternate exterior angles will be congruent.

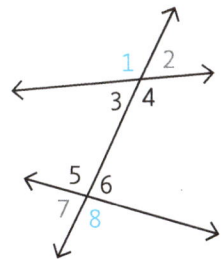

1 and 8 are alternate exterior angles. 2 and 7 are also alternate exterior angles.

ALTERNATE INTERIOR ANGLES

When two straight lines are cut by a third line called a transversal, the pairs of angles formed inside the two lines and on the opposite sides of the transversal are called Alternate Interior Angles.

Note: If two parallel lines are cut by a transversal, the alternate interior angles will be congruent.

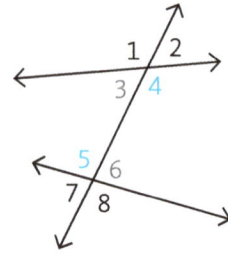

3 and 6 are alternate interior angles. 4 and 5 are also alternate interior angles.

ALTITUDE

1) In a polygon, the distance from the base to the farthest point on the perimeter.

In a triangle, the altitude is the length of a line segment perpendicular to its base, from that base to the opposite angle. Parallelograms, including squares and rectangles, have two altitudes which depend on the side chosen for the base.

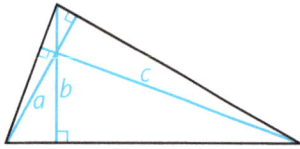

Triangles have three altitudes, which depend on the side chosen for the base. *a*, *b* and *c* are the altitudes of this triangle.

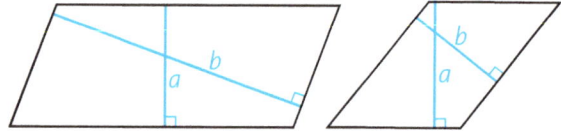

a and *b* are the altitudes of these parallelograms.

2) In a solid, the distance from the base to the highest point.

In three dimensional figures, such as pyramids or cones, the altitude is a perpendicular line segment between the base and the vertex. The altitude of the cylinder is a perpendicular line segment from the plane of one base to the plane of the other.

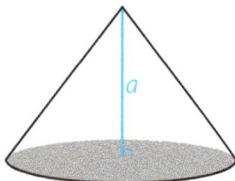

Cone

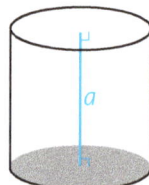

Right cylinder

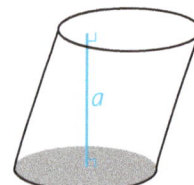

Oblique cylinder

(See HEIGHT)

ANALYTIC GEOMETRY

A branch of mathematics that uses algebra to study geometric figures, defining geometric figures in algebraic equations.

ANGLE

In a plane, the figure formed by two rays that have a common endpoint or by two straight lines or line segments which intersect. The intersection of 2 lines creates 4 angles.

The common endpoint of rays or the point of intersection of lines is the vertex of the angles.

Angles are measured in degrees.

(See DEGREE, RAY)

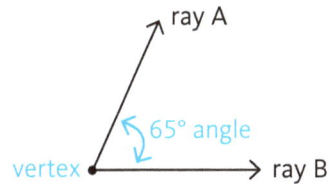

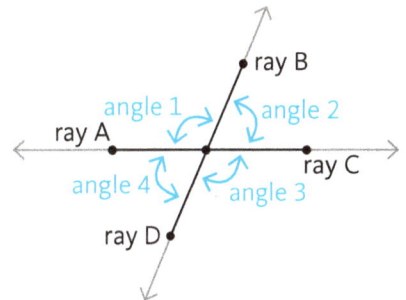

The rays that form these 4 angles are contained on the two lines.

ANNULUS

The region between two concentric circles.

The area in blue is an annulus.

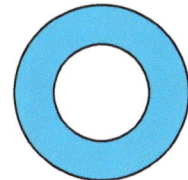

APEX

The vertex or highest point of a pyramid or a cone measured by a straight line segment perpendicular to the base.

(See CONE, PYRAMID)

APPROXIMATE

Almost the same as or nearly equal to.

Example: An acre has approximately the same area as a football field.

APPROXIMATION

When two numbers are very close to each other, one may sometimes be substituted for the other to make calculations easier. In this case, the result of the calculations would be an approximation.

Example: When calculating the area of a circle, π is often given as 3.1416, but π is really the irrational number 3.1415926536.... π is also often approximated as $\frac{22}{7}$. Using 3.1416 or $\frac{22}{7}$ results in a very close, but not exact, answer or an approximation.

ARC

The part of a curve between two given points on the curve.

Example: An arc of a circle is the section of the circle that lies between two given points.

Two points on a circle define two arcs and usually one is longer and one is shorter. If the points are at the end of a diameter, the arcs are equal.

Points A and B on this circle define two arcs. The longer would be referred to as the *major arc AB*, the shorter as the *minor arc AB*.

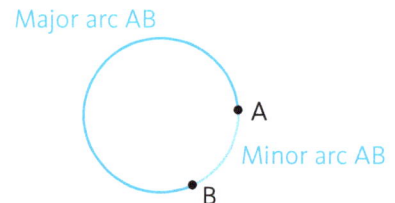

Major arc AB

A

Minor arc AB

B

ARCHIMEDEAN SOLIDS

Polyhedrons that have regular polygons for each of their faces. Two or more different polygons appear in each of the Archimedean solids, unlike the Platonic Solids which have faces of only one single type of polygon. In an Archimedean solid, the same polygons appear in the exact same sequence around every vertex.

Example: In this truncated tetrahedron, the polygons are 4 regular hexagons and 4 equilateral triangles.

Truncated tetrahedron

(See PLATONIC SOLIDS, POLYGONS, POLYHEDRONS)

ARCHIMEDES

A Greek mathematician who lived from 290 BCE to 211 BCE. Archimedes studied in Alexandria and lived and worked in Syracuse, on the island of Sicily, which was a Greek colony at the time. Archimedes developed formulas to compute the surface area and volume of a sphere and the circumference of a circle and developed the principle of floating bodies. He is said to have also designed military machines that delayed the Romans from capturing his city.

AREA

The space enclosed by a plane figure; the measure of the section of a plane enclosed by a figure on the plane. Area is given in square units.

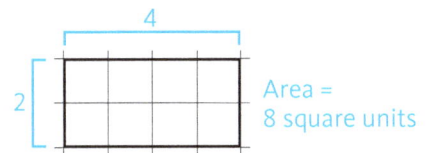

The formula to find the area of a rectangle is Base × Height = Area.

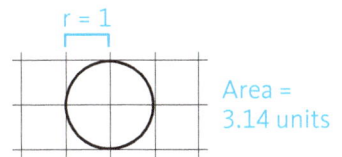

The formula to find the area of a circle is πr^2 = Area.

The formula to find the area of a triangle is $\frac{1}{2}$ Base × Height = Area.

Area = 8 square units

Area = 3.14 units

Area = 4 units

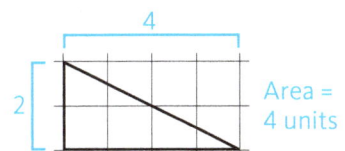

(See SQUARE UNIT)

AREA MODEL for MULTIPLICATION

A rectangular array used to represent a multiplication equation. The dimensions of the rectangle represent the factors in the multiplication and the area of the rectangle represents the product.

Example: The area of the rectangle is 20 square units. It represents the equation 4 × 5 = 20.

ARITHMETIC

A branch of mathematics that studies the four basic operations on numbers: addition; subtraction; multiplication; division.

(See BASIC OPERATIONS)

ARITHMETIC MEAN

A method to determine the center of a set of numbers; the average of a set of numbers. To find the arithmetic mean, first find the sum of all the numbers in a set and then divide this sum by the number of members in the set that you have added together.

Example: The arithmetic mean of the following group of 7 numbers, 2, 4, 5, 7, 8, 8, 9 is:
2 + 4 + 5 + 7 + 8 + 8 + 9 = 42
42 ÷ 7 = 6
6 is the arithmetic mean

The average of a set of numbers does not have to be one of the numbers in the set.

(See AVERAGE)

ARITHEMETIC PROGRESSION

(See ARITHMETIC SEQUENCE)

ARITHMETIC SEQUENCE

A number pattern in which there is a constant difference between consecutive members. Arithmetic sequences are sometimes called arithmetic progressions or arithmetic patterns. *Arithmetic patterns is the term that is used in CCSS.*

Examples: The set of even numbers form an arithmetic sequence with the common difference of 2: 2, 4, 6, 8 ...

3, 6, 9, 12, 15... an arithmetic sequence with a common difference of 3.

(See COMMON DIFFERENCE, NUMBER PATTERN)

ARRAY

An orderly arrangement in rows and columns; an arrangement of numbers in columns and rows.

Arrays are often used to display the results of ordered arithmetic operations.

(See TABLE)

An array of dots

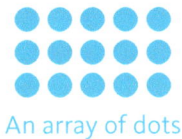

x	1	2	3	4	5	6	7
1	1	2	3	4	5	6	7
2	2	4	6	8	10	12	14
3	3	6	9	12	15	18	21
4	4	8	12	16	20	24	28
5	5	10	15	20	25	30	35
6	6	12	18	24	30	36	42
7	7	14	21	28	35	42	49

An array displaying the multiplication of numbers 1 through 7.

ASSOCIATIVE PROPERTY

One of the three properties of operations, an arithmetic operation obeys the associative property if the grouping of the numbers used in the operation does not change the results of the operation.

Addition and multiplication obey the associative property; subtraction and division do not.

Associative Property of Addition: a + (b + c) = (a + b) + c
Associative Property of Multiplication: a × (b × c) = (a × b) × c

Examples of the associative properties of addition and multiplication.
2 + (8 + 3) = 13   (2 + 8) + 3 = 13   2 × (8 × 3) = (2 × 8) × 3 = 48

(See COMMUTATIVE PROPERTY, DISTRIBUTIVE PROPERTY)

ASYMMETRY

Describes a figure that is not symmetrical about a line or a point.

Example: Any figure divided into two unequal halves is asymmetric.

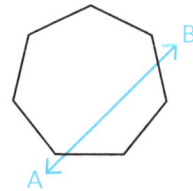

This figure is asymmetric across line AB

(See SYMMETRY)

ATTRIBUTE

A characteristic or quality that describes something. Attributes are used to define members of a set in the collection and categorization of data.

Examples of attributes are size, shape, color or number.

(See DATA, SET THEORY)

ATTRIBUTE PATTERN

Objects arranged according to specified attributes.

Examples of attribute patterns:

(See ATTRIBUTE, PATTERN)

AVERAGE

The same as the arithmetic mean, it is a number that is often used to represent a large group of numbers.

Example: The average income in the country for that year was $50,000.

Note: A MEDIAN or MODE might also be used in place of an average.

(See ARITHMETIC MEAN, MEDIAN, MODE)

AXIOM

A statement that is assumed to be true without proof; a fact that is self-evident.

Example: Things equal to the same thing are also equal to one another:
If A = B and B = C then A = C.

AXIS

1) The straight line around which an object or image revolves.

2) A reference line in the Cartesian coordinate system. The horizontal number line is commonly called the x axis and the vertical number line is called the y axis.

Note: The method of assigning positions to points in a plane is called a coordinate system. In the Cartesian system, intersecting number lines are used to create a rectangular grid, and positions on that grid are defined by their position in relation to both number lines. The horizontal number line is commonly called the x axis and the vertical number line is called the y axis.

Example: Using this coordinate system we would locate the point (3, 2), meaning that it is located at a distance of 3 from 0 along the x axis and 2 from zero along the y axis.

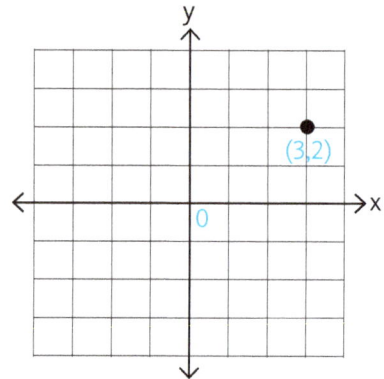

(See CARTESIAN COORDINATE SYSTEM, ORDERED PAIRS)

AXIS OF SYMMETRY

A line that divides a figure into two symmetrical parts. The axis of symmetry divides the figure in such a way that the part of the figure on one side of the line is the mirror image of the part of the figure on the other side. The axis of symmetry is also called a line of symmetry.

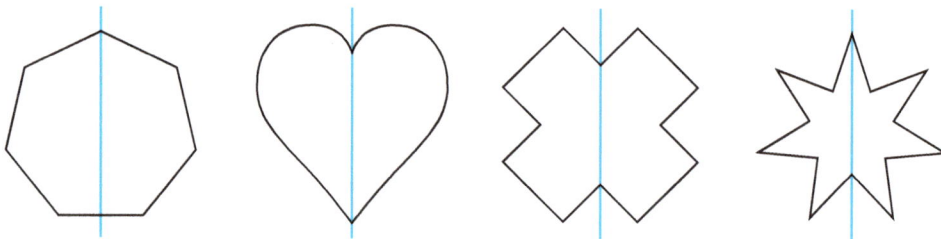

(See SYMMETRY)

B

BAR GRAPH

A diagram that gives a visual representation for data. Bar graphs, sometimes called bar charts, allow us to compare categories of information.

Bar graphs can be arranged vertically: Or horizontally:

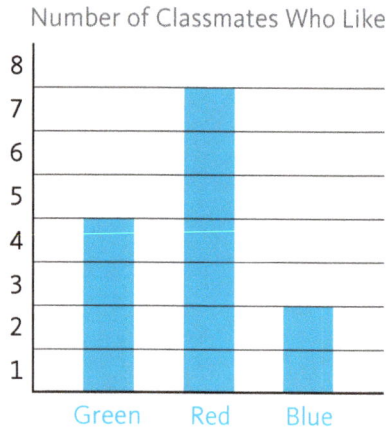

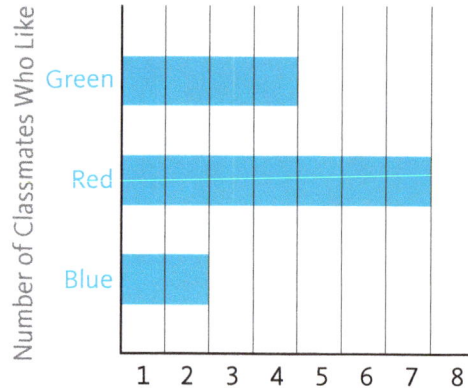

Number of Classmates Who Like

BAR MODEL

(See TAPE DIAGRAM)

BASE
Note: There are four definitions.

1) In geometry, the base of a plane figure or polygon is one of the sides of the polygon and is frequently displayed as the side on which the polygon rests. The base of a shape can be any side that forms a right angle with a line that determines its height.

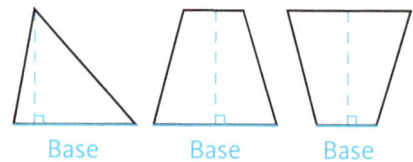

Base   Base   Base

2) The base of a solid figure is one of the faces and in images is usually displayed as the face on which the solid figure rests.

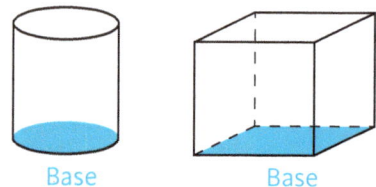

Base   Base

continued ⟶

3) In a place value system of numeration, the base is the number of unique digits used in that system.

Example: In the base 10 or decimal system that we use, there are 10 digits: 0, 1, 2, 3, 4, 5, 6, 7, 8, and 9. By using place value, these digits can represent any number. The value of each position is equal to the powers of the base, in this case 10. In a number written in base 10 the first position to the left of the decimal represents 1. The second position represents 10. The third position represents 100, or 10 to the second power. The fourth position represents 1000 or 10 to the third power. Thus 4872 in base ten represents:

$$4 \times 1000 \qquad 8 \times 100 \qquad 7 \times 10 \qquad 2 \times 1$$

Using the base with only three digits, 0, 1, and 2, each position would represent powers of 3. In base 3 the first position to the left of the decimal represents 1. The second position represents 3. The third position represents 9, or 3 to the second power. The fourth position represents 27 or 3 to the third power. Thus 2102 in base three represents:

$$2 \times 27 \qquad 1 \times 9 \qquad 0 \times 3 \qquad 2 \times 1$$
2102 in base 3 is equal to 64 in base 10.

(See BINARY NUMBER, PLACE VALUE, POWER)

4) A number that is raised to a power. Exponents are a simple way of writing the repeated multiplication of a number by itself.

Examples: In exponential notation 4^2 simply means 4×4, and 5^3 means $5 \times 5 \times 5$.
$4^2 = 4 \times 4 = 16 \qquad 5^3 = 5 \times 5 \times 5 = 125$

In general algebraic notation, X^n means X used as a factor n times.

In exponential notation, the number that is multiplied by itself is called the base, and the number of times that number is multiplied is written as the exponent.

(See EXPONENTIAL NOTATION, POWER)

BASIC FACTS

In arithmetic, the results of performing the four basic operations of addition, subtraction, multiplication and division on the digits of base ten are considered fundamental facts, which should be remembered and easily recalled. These basic facts are often arranged in arrays or tables to enable students to quickly learn the combinations of digits.

BASIC OPERATION

There are four basic operations of arithmetic: addition; subtraction; multiplication; and division.

BETWEEN

In geometry, a point lies between two other points if it lies on the line connecting those points and has one of the points to either side.

On this line, point B lies between points A and C.

BILLION

A billion is equal to 1000 million or $1,000,000 \times 1,000 = 1,000,000,000$.

In exponential notation, one billion is equal to 10 to the ninth power or 10^9.

BINARY NUMBERS

Numbers written in a place value system that uses only two digits: 0 and 1. When using a base with only two digits, each position must represent a power of 2.

In base 2 the first position to the left of the decimal represents 1 or 2^0. The second position represents 2 or 2^1. The third position represents 2 to the second power or 2^2 (4). The fourth position represents 2 to the third power or 2^3 (8).

continued ———→

Example: The number 101010 in base two is equal to

1×32
0×16
1×8
0×4
1×2
0×1
Or 42 in base 10.

Numbers written in binary notation are much longer and more cumbersome in calculations than numbers written in decimal notation. Note the above number expressed in different bases:

| 101010 | 42 |
| binary notation or base 2 | decimal notation or base 10 |

(See BASE definition 3, PLACE VALUE, POWER)

BISECT

To partition a geometric figure into two equal parts.

To cut in half.

Point D bisects line segment $\overline{AB}$
if AD = DB

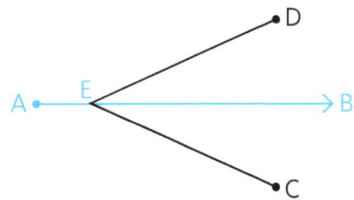

Ray $\overrightarrow{AB}$ bisects angle CED
if CEB = BED

BIVARIATE DATA

Pairs of linked numerical observations often represented on a scatter plot.

Note: Bivariate data has two variables, and the values of these variables are often related. When the data is represented on a scatter plot, any relationship between the variables can be seen.

Examples: A list of the heights and shoe sizes for each student in a school.

The temperature in a town for several days and the use of electricity on each day.

(See SCATTER PLOT)

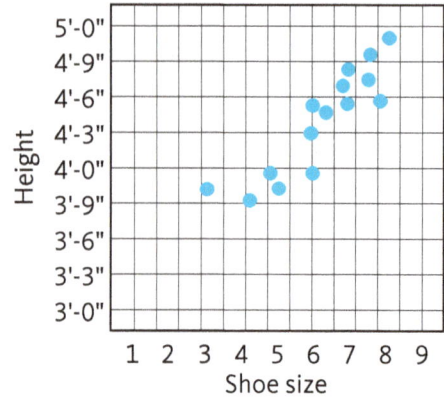

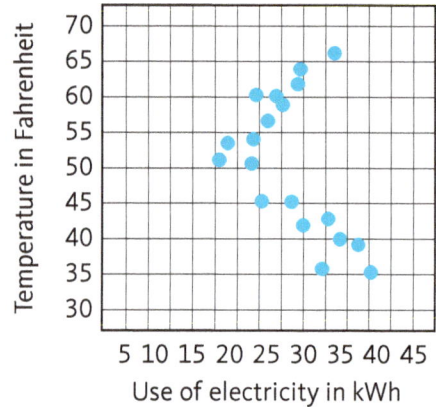

BOOLEAN ALGEBRA

The study of operations performed on variables that can have only one of two values: 0 and 1.

Boolean algebra is important is the study of logic because statements are classified in two ways, true or false; and in computer science because computers only recognize two states, on and off, recognized as 1 and 0.

Boolean algebra was developed by English mathematician George Boole (1815-1865).

BOX PLOT

A method of visually displaying a distribution of data along a number line by using the median, quartiles, and extremes of the data set. Quartiles divide the data into four equal parts and a box is drawn around the two middle quartiles with the first and last quartiles extending beyond the box. A box plot is sometimes called a box and whisker plot because the first and last quartile extensions resemble whiskers.

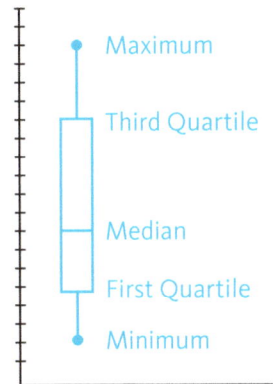

Using a box and whisker plot we can see the spread of the values.

(See FIVE NUMBER SUMMARY)

29

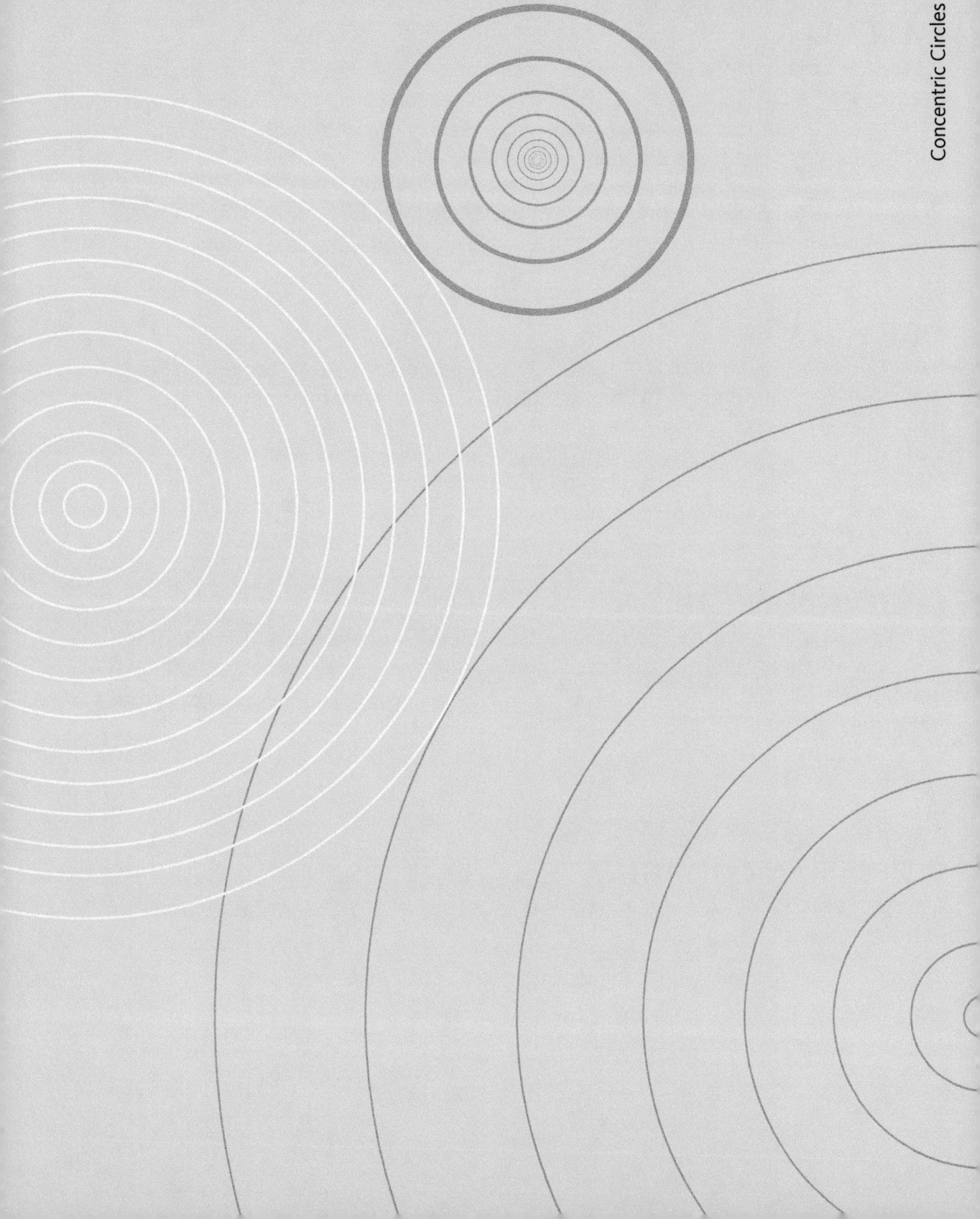

CALCULUS

A branch of mathematics that studies rates of change. There are two main branches of calculus: Differential calculus and integral calculus. Differential calculus determines the rate of change of a quantity; integral calculus finds the quantity when the rate of change is known.

Calculus was developed in the late seventeenth century by two mathematicians working independently of each other, Isaac Newton and Gottfried Leibniz.

CAPACITY

In mathematics, the measure of the amount of a liquid that a container can hold when full. Capacity is given in units of liquid measure: cups; quarts; gallons; milliliters; liters; etc.

The word capacity is often used to denote other measurements, such as the number of people a theatre can hold.

CARDINAL NUMBERS

Numbers used to measure the size of sets; numbers that show quantity. Cardinal numbers are often referred to as the counting numbers because they are the numbers we use to tell 'how many'. Note: Cardinal numbers indicate quantity, but not order.

Example: A baseball team has 9 players.

CARTESIAN COORDINATE SYSTEM

A system used to indicate the positions of points on a two-dimensional surface or in three-dimensional space.

continued ⟶

A Cartesian frame consists of two perpendicular axes that cross at a central point called the origin. These axes are basically number lines. Positions are determined according to their distance from the origin or intersection of the lines.

Cartesian three-space, sometimes called an xyz -space, has a third axis at right angles to the two dimensional plane.

The coordinate system is named for the French mathematician and philosopher René Descartes (1596-1650). Descartes' breakthrough was to take two number lines, stand one up on its end, and have it cross the first number line at zero.

(See AXIS, COORDINATES, ORDERED PAIRS)

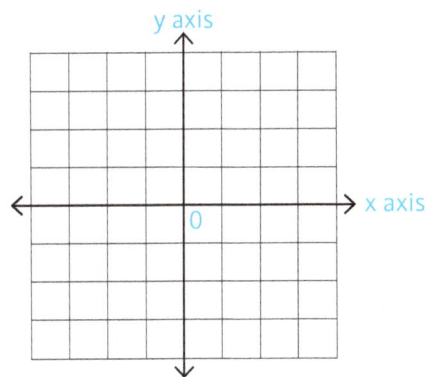

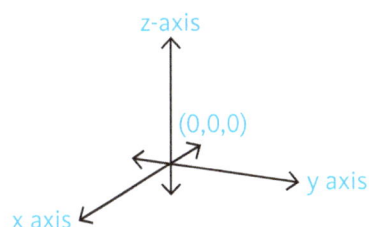

CELSIUS TEMPERATURE SCALE

The scale used to measure temperature in the metric system. The scale sets the freezing point of water at 0° Celsius and the boiling point of water at sea-level at 100° Celsius. It is also called the centigrade scale because there are 100 degrees (standard measurement units) between freezing and boiling water.

CENT

A unit of money in the United States, a cent is equal to $\frac{1}{100}$ of a dollar. The symbol for cent is ¢.

(See MONEY)

CENTER

Of a circle: The point inside the circle that is equidistant from all points on the circle.

Of an ellipse: The point inside the ellipse where the two axes of symmetry intersect.

Of a sphere: A point at the center that is the equidistant from all points on the sphere.

Of a regular polygon: The point at the center of the circle that can be inscribed in that polygon.

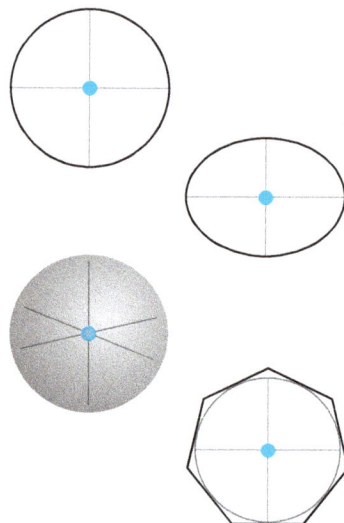

CENTRAL ANGLE

An angle that has its vertex at the center of a circle.

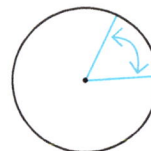

CENTI-

A prefix meaning one hundredth ($\frac{1}{100}$). In the metric measuring system 'centi' is a prefix used to denote 100 units.

CENTIGRADE SCALE

(See CELSIUS SCALE)

CENTIGRAM

A unit of weight in the metric measurement system.

Note: In the metric system 'centi' is a prefix for 100 units. A centigram is one hundredth ($\frac{1}{100}$) of a gram. Abbreviation: cg

100 centigrams = 1 gram

CENTILITER

A unit of capacity in the metric measurement system. Abbreviation: cl

Note: In the metric system 'centi' is a prefix for 100 units.

100 centiliters = 1 liter

CENTIMETER

A unit of length in the metric measurement system. Abbreviation: cm

Note: In the metric system 'centi' is a prefix for 100 units.

100 centimeters = 1 meter

CENTROID

The center of mass of an object. It is the point within the object where the object would balance if it were supported by only one support.

CHAOS THEORY

The study of systems that have the property that a small change in the initial conditions of the system leads to very large changes in the system as it evolves. Even though future behavior within the system is determined by the initial conditions, and no random elements are involved, this property makes long-term predictions about the system impossible.

CHORD

A line segment within a circle that has both endpoints on the circle.

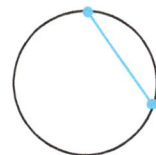

(See DIAMETER)

CIRCLE

A closed curve in a plane with every point on the curve an equal distance from a given point which is the center of the circle.

The distance from the center of a circle to all the points that form the circle is called the radius of the circle; every circle can be defined by its center and the length of its radius. The diameter of a circle is a line segment that connects two points on the circle and passes through its center; the diameter of a circle is equal to twice the length of its radius.

Circle: A 2-dimensional curve with all points the same distance from a central point.

(See ANNULUS, DIAMETER, RADIUS)

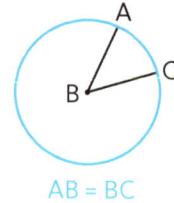

AB = BC

CIRCLE GRAPH

A graph in the shape of a circle which shows the way a total amount is divided.

If a finite set is divided into subsets and each subset is defined as a percentage of the entire set, a circle graph is a good way to visually display the data.

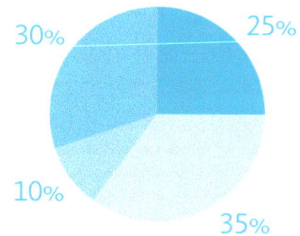

Circle graphs are also called pie charts.

CIRCUMFERENCE

The total distance around a curve; the length measured around a closed curve.

Note: The circumference of a circle is slightly longer than 3 times its diameter. The actual ratio between the diameter and the circumference of a circle is the number represented by π which is the irrational number 3.14159… To find the circumference of any circle, multiply the diameter of the circle by π.

Circumference = π × diameter or $C = \pi \times d$

continued ⟶

For this circle with a diameter of 5, the circumference is C = π × 5 = 15.70795... or approximately 15.708

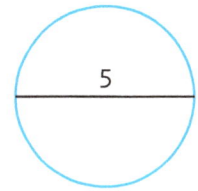

Because the radius of a circle is $\frac{1}{2}$ the length of the diameter, often the formula for finding the circumference is given using the radius: C = 2πr

(See DIAMETER, PERIMETER, PI π)

CIRCUMSCRIBE

To construct a geometric figure around a different geometric figure so that all vertices touch or as many points as possible touch.

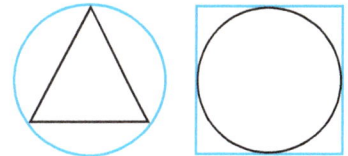

Example: A circle circumscribed around a triangle and a square circumscribed around a circle.

CLASSIFY

To sort or organize by attributes or characteristics.

Example: Triangles may be classified by their angle measures or by their side lengths.

CLOSED CURVE

A curve that completely encloses an area in a plane; a curve in a plane that flows continually with no gap and might be thought of as beginning and ending at any same point on that curve.

Circles and ellipses are examples of simple closed curves, but note that despite the name 'curve', a simple closed curve does not actually have to curve.

Note: Polygons fit the definition of closed curves.

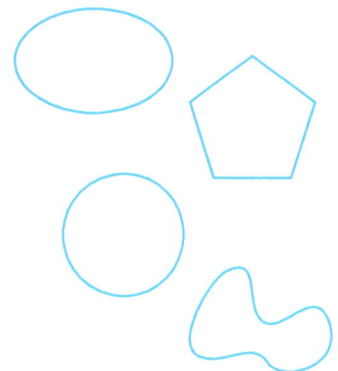

COEFFICIENT

A number used to multiply a variable, usually within an algebraic expression. In a polynomial, the coefficients are the numbers that are immediately in front of the variables.

Examples: 5n means 5 times n. The quantity n is a variable and 5 is a coefficient. In the polynomial $2x + 3y + 8$, 2 and 3 are coefficients.

(See POLYNOMIAL, VARIABLE)

COLLINEAR

Points are collinear if a straight line passes through them. That is, if a set of points all lie in a straight line, they are called 'collinear'.

(See POINT)

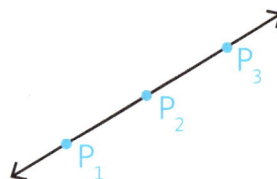

P_1, P_2, P_3 are collinear

COLUMN

A vertical arrangement of data in an array or a table.

Note: In tables and arrays, data is arranged in rows (horizontally or side to side) and columns (vertically or top to bottom).

(See ARRAY, MATRIX, TABLE)

COMMON DENOMINATOR

A number that is a multiple of all the denominators of a set of fractions. Note that the common denominator of any set of fractions can be divided by any of the denominators without leaving a remainder.

Example: $\frac{1}{2}, \frac{1}{3}$, and $\frac{1}{4}$ have a common denominator of 12.

COMMON DIFFERENCE

The constant difference in an arithmetic sequence or in any number pattern in which there is an equal difference between consecutive members.

Example: 3, 6, 9, 12, 15....
In this sequence, 3 is the common difference.

COMMON DIVISOR

A number that is a factor of each member of a group of numbers.

Example: 3 is a common divisor (and factor) of 9, 15 and 21.

Also called COMMON FACTOR

COMMON FACTOR

A number that is a factor of each member of a group of numbers.

5 is a common factor of 10 and 25.

COMMON MULTIPLE

A multiple that two or more numbers share.

Examples:
2, 4, 6, 8, 10, 12.... are multiples of 2; 3, 6, 9, 12....are multiples of 3.
6, 12 are common multiples of 2 and 3.

COMMUTATIVE PROPERTY

One of the three basic properties of operations, it states that when adding or multiplying numbers, the order in which the numbers are added or multiplied does not change the result. Sometimes it is referred to as the commutative law.

Commutative property of addition: a + b = b + a

Commutative property of multiplication: a × b = b × a

Examples of the commutative properties of addition and multiplication:
8 + 3 = 3 + 8 = 11   8 × 3 = 3 × 8 = 24

Note: Though addition and multiplication are commutative operations, subtraction and division are not commutative.

Example: 3 – 8 ≠ 8 – 3   and   3 ÷ 8 ≠ 8 ÷ 3

(*See ASSOCIATIVE PROPERTY, DISTRIBUTIVE PROPERTY*)

COMPASS

A device composed of two adjustable legs, it is used to draw circles and arcs and to copy or measure line segments.

Many plane figures can be constructed using a compass and a straightedge.

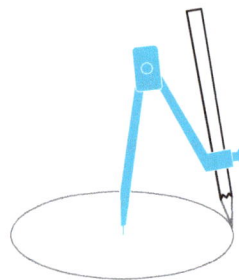

COMPATIBLE NUMBERS

Numbers that replace some or all of the original numbers in a mathematical expression in order to make computation easier. The result of using compatible numbers is usually an estimate, not an exact answer.

Examples: In the division expression 49 ÷ 3, we could adjust 49 to 48. 48 ÷ 3 is 16, so a reasonable estimate for 49 ÷ 3 is 16.

In the addition expression 28 + 43, we could adjust the addends so that the expression is 25 + 45. 25 + 45 is 70, so a reasonable estimate for 28 + 43 is 70.

COMPLEX FRACTION

A fraction, $\frac{A}{B}$, in which A and/or B are also fractions.

Examples: $\dfrac{\frac{2}{3}}{\frac{3}{8}}$ $\dfrac{9}{\frac{5}{8}}$ $\dfrac{\frac{1}{8}}{7}$

COMPLEMENT OF A SET

The complement of a set, set A, is a set composed of all the elements that are part of a universal set, U, that are not included in set A. That is, the set composed of all elements within the universal set that are not included in set A is the compliment of set A.

If the universal set is the set of all positive integers, and set A is the set of all even integers, then the compliment of set A would be the set of all odd integers.

(See UNIVERSAL SET)

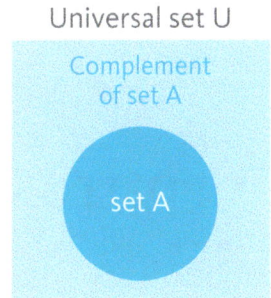

Universal set U

Complement of set A

set A

COMPLEMENT OF AN ANGLE

One angle that when added to another makes a 90° angle.

If two angles added together form a right angle (a 90° angle) they are complements of each other.

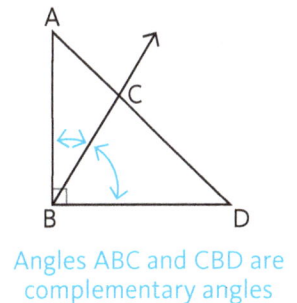

Angles ABC and CBD are complementary angles

COMPOSE

To combine or to put together. In geometry, figures can be joined together to form other figures. A number can be composed by combining quantities (or parts) to form the whole.

Examples: In geometry, figures can be joined together to form other figures. In this example, a triangle and a square are put together to form a pentagon.

4392 is composed of 4 thousands, 3 hundreds, 9 tens and 2 units.

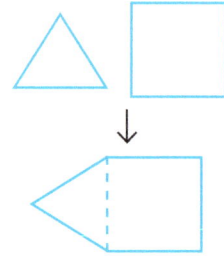

COMPOSITE NUMBER

A positive integer with more than two factors; a natural number that is not a prime number or equal to 1.

A composite number can be expressed as the product of two natural numbers other than itself and 1.

Examples: 6, 14, 27, 36 are all composite numbers.

COMPOUND INTEREST

Interest paid on both the principal that was initially invested and on the interest already earned on that principal. This also applies to an amount owed, or a debt. The interest owed on credit card debt is compound interest; unpaid interest from a period is added to the debt.

Example: In compound interest, the interest earned in one interest period is added to the investment before calculating interest for the next interest period. If you invested $100 in a bank and the bank pays 2% compound interest annually, at the end of the first year, your account balance would be:
$100 + (2% of $100) = $100 + $2 = $102.

continued ⟶

For the second year, $102 is now the principal, and the interest will be paid on this amount. That means that the interest for the second year will be calculated on the principal $102.

$102 + (2% of $102) = $102 + $2.04 = $104.04.

COMPUTATION ALGORITHM

A set of predefined steps for simplifying mathematical expressions that gives the correct result in every case when the steps are carried out correctly.

In the CCSS it is defined as the set of predefined steps applicable to a class of problems that give the correct result in every case.

(See ALGORITHM)

COMPUTATION STRATEGY

Purposeful manipulations that may be chosen to simplify mathematical expressions. Strategies may not have a fixed order and may be aimed at converting one mathematical statement into another.

CONCAVE

1) The common meaning is 'curved inward', like the inner surface of a bowl or the inner surface of a sphere.

2) In mathematics, a polygon is concave if there are points on the perimeter of the figure that can be joined by a line segment that is outside the figure. When at least one of the interior angles of a polygon is greater than 180°, it will be a concave. Note: If you can draw a line through a polygon that will intersect more than two lines of the perimeter of the polygon, then the polygon is concave.

Note how A) it is possible to draw a line segment outside the polygon that connects points on its perimeter and B) it is possible to draw a line through each of these examples and have the line intersect the perimeter in more than 2 places.

A)

B)

(See CONVEX)

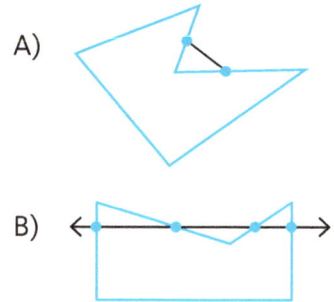

CONCENTRIC CIRCLES

Circles that have the same center but different diameters.

Example: A dart board features concentric circles.

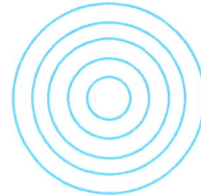

CONE

A three-dimensional figure that has a closed curve as its base and has its vertex in another plane.

Example: The shape of an ice cream cone.

Right Cone: A right cone is a cone in which the vertex is aligned directly above the center of the base. The base does not have to be a circle but could be, for example, an ellipse.

Right Circular Cone: When the base of a right cone is a circle, it is called a right circular cone. In a right circular cone, each point on the circle at the base is equidistant from the vertex of the cone.

(See APEX, BASE, CLOSED CURVE, VERTEX)

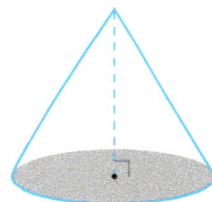
Right circular cone

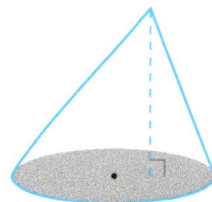
Oblique circular cone

CONGRUENT

Having exactly the same shape and size.

Two plane or solid figures are congruent if one can be obtained from the other by rigid motion, meaning by a sequence of rotations, reflections, and/or translations.

In the CCSS, two geometric figures are defined to be congruent if there is a sequence of rigid motions that carries one onto the other, meaning that shapes are congruent if you can rotate, flip and/or slide one to fit exactly over the other.

Congruent triangles

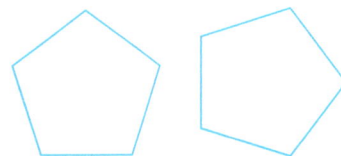
Congruent polygons

CONIC SECTION

A curve created by having a plane slice through a cone.

By taking different slices through a cone you can create the four different conic sections: a circle; an ellipse; a parabola; or a hyperbola.

(See CIRCLE, ELLIPSE, HYPERBOLA, PARABOLA)

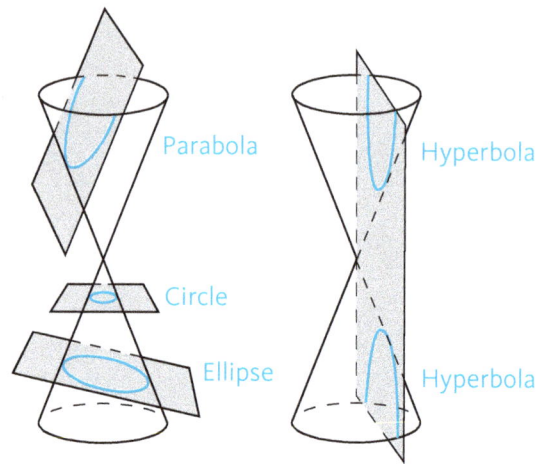

CONSTANT

A fixed value; a quantity that does not change.

In an algebraic expression or equation, the constant term has a fixed value and does not contain variables. A constant can be a numeral or can be represented by a letter or a symbol.

Examples: In the polynomial $3x + 8$, 8 is a constant.

The formula for finding the area of a circle is $A = \pi r^2$, where A is the Area of the circle and r is the radius. The Greek letter π represents the constant 3.1415.....

CONSTRUCTION

A drawing of a geometric figure made using only a compass and a straightedge.

(See COMPASS, STRAIGHTEDGE)

CONVEX

1) The common meaning of convex is 'curved outward', like the outer surface of a bowl or the outer surface of a sphere.

2) A polygon is convex if any line segment joining points on the perimeter of the polygon must be inside the polygon, and any line drawn through the polygon will intersect no more than two lines on the perimeter of the polygon.

Note how A) any line segment that connects points on its perimeter must be inside the polygon and B) it is not possible to draw a line through any of these examples and have the line intersect the perimeter in more than 2 places. Try it!

A)

B)

(See CONCAVE)

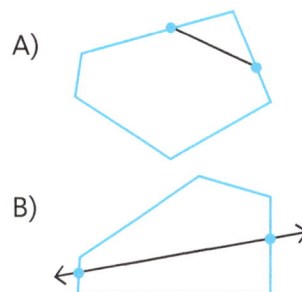

COORDINATE SYSTEM

One of several different methods used to define the position of a point.

(See CARTESIAN COORDINATE SYSTEM, POLAR COORDINATE SYSTEM)

COORDINATES (COORDINATE PAIR)

An ordered set of numbers used to name the exact location of a point on a coordinate system such as a Cartesian coordinate system.

In a Cartesian coordinate system in a plane, an ordered pair of numbers is used to locate a point. The first number gives the distance along the horizontal axis (often called the x axis) and the second number shows the distance up or down the vertical axis (often called the y axis).

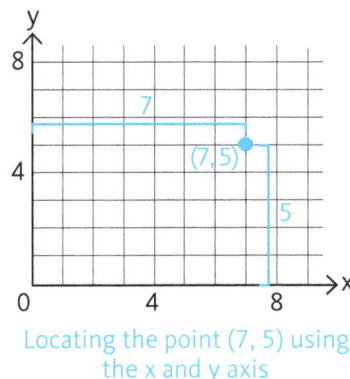

Locating the point (7, 5) using the x and y axis

continued ⟶

COORDINATES (COORDINATE PAIR) CONTINUED

In a polar coordinate system, the same axis is used to locate points, but points are named by distance from the origin and an angle of inclination.

In a three dimensional coordinate system a third axis is added and an ordered set of three numbers is used to locate a point. You might picture this third axis as going above and below the page.

(See CARTESIAN COORDINATE SYSTEM, ORDERED PAIR, POLAR COORDINATE SYSTEM, QUADRANT)

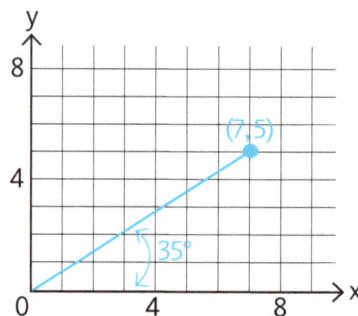

Locating the same point using polar coordinate system

COPLANAR

To lie in the same plane.

For example, the vertices of a triangle lie in the same plane, but the base of a pyramid and its vertex do not lie in the same plane.

CORRELATION

(See TREND LINE)

CORRESPONDING ANGLES

1) When two lines are intersected by a third line, the intersection forms two sets of angles. The angles in the same position are called corresponding angles.

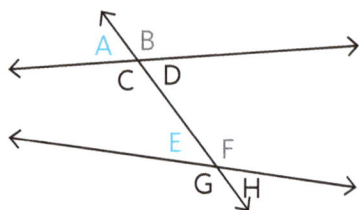

A and E are corresponding angles.
B and F are corresponding angles.

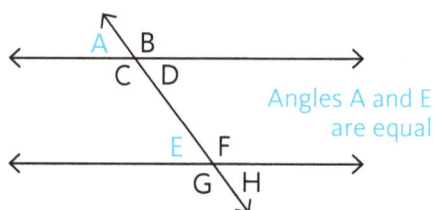

Angles A and E are equal

If the two lines that are crossed are parallel lines, then the corresponding angles will be equal.

continued ⟶

2) Angles that are in the same position in two congruent or similar shapes are corresponding angles.

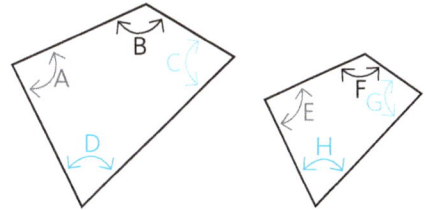

Angles, A and E; B and F, C and G and D and H are corresponding angles.

CORRESPONDING SIDES
Sides that are in the same position in two congruent or similar shapes.

Note: In similar polygons all corresponding angles are congruent and all corresponding sides are proportional.

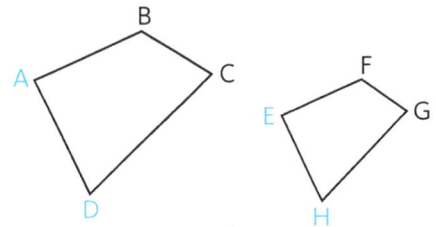

AD and EH are corresponding sides.

COSINE
In a right triangle, the length of the side adjacent to an angle divided by the length of the hypotenuse. Cosine is usually abbreviated as cos. COS α = adjacent ÷ hypotenuse.

Note: The cosine of an angle is a constant because the sides of all right triangles are in proportion depending on the other two angles.

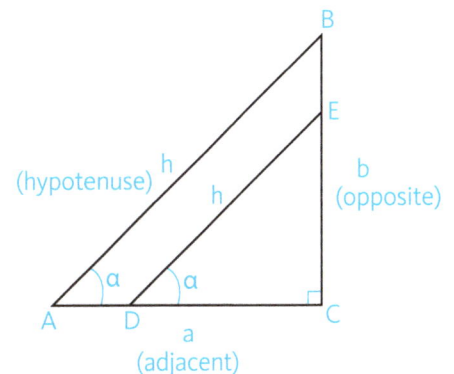

Example: The cosine of angle CAB is the same as the cosine of angle CDE.

(See TRIGONOMETRIC FUNCTIONS)

COUNTING BACK

A strategy used to find a missing addend in an open addition sentence or a difference in a subtraction open sentence. Counting back often involves using a number line or number chart. We could also count back mentally or using our fingers.

Examples: $3 + x = 8$ $9 - 5 = x$

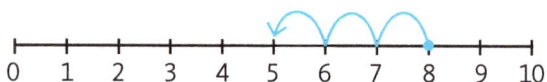

Start at the sum, 8, and count back 3 places on the number line to find the missing addend, 5.

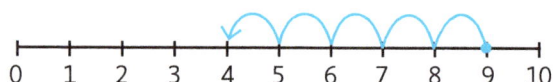

Start at the minuend, 9, and count back 5 places on the number line to find the difference, 4.

COUNTING NUMBERS

The same as the natural numbers, they are the numbers used to count: 1, 2, 3, 4, 5...∞

Note: Zero is not included in the set of counting numbers.

(See WHOLE NUMBERS)

COUNTING ON

A strategy for finding the number of objects in a group without having to count every member of the group.

For example, if a stack of books is known to have 5 books and 3 more books are added, it is not necessary to count the stack of 5 again. One can find the total by counting on—pointing to the top book and saying 'five' and then following with 'six, seven, eight'.

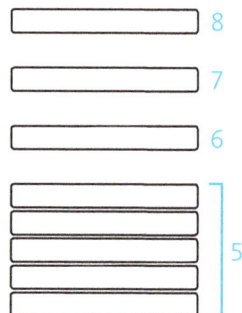

CREDIT

In an accounting system, something that is received and that will be added. It is the opposite of a debit.

CUBE

1) A solid figure with six congruent (exactly equal) square faces. A cube has eight vertices and twelve edges. A cube is one of the five regular polyhedral.

2) The cube of a number is that number used as a factor 3 times. The cube of any number, A, is written as A^3, and is equal to $A \times A \times A$. The number to be used as a factor is called the base.

The faces are all congruent. The vertices and the edges are equal.

Example: 2 cubed, or the base 2 raised to the third power, is written as 2^3. $2^3 = 2 \times 2 \times 2 = 8$

(See BASE, POWER, REGULAR POLYHEDRAL, VOLUME)

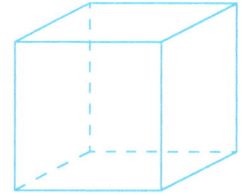

CUBE ROOT

The cube root of a number is another number that, when used as a factor three times yields the number

Example: 3 is the cube root of 27 because $3 \times 3 \times 3 = 27$. 4 is the cube root of 64 because $4^3 = 64$: $4 \times 4 \times 4 = 64$

(See BASE, POWER)

CUBIC

A cubic unit is a measure of volume.

Volume is the measure of the amount of space inside a solid figure, such as the space inside a rectangular solid, a cylinder or even a ball. Volume is a measurement in three dimensions: height, length, depth. The volume of any solid is measured in Cubic Units.

Note: To measure volume we use a standard cube whose edge is of a stated length. Volume is the measurement of how many of these standard cubic units fit inside the figure we are measuring.
Examples of standard cubic units would be a cubic foot that is a cube with edges that are exactly one foot in length; or a cubic centimeter, which is a cube with edges that are exactly one centimeter in length.

A cubic centimeter is a cube with edges that measure 1 centimeter. Each face of the cube measures 1 square centimeter. The volume of the cube is 1 cubic centimeter. To measure the volume of a three dimensional object, we would determine how many cubic centimeters fit inside.

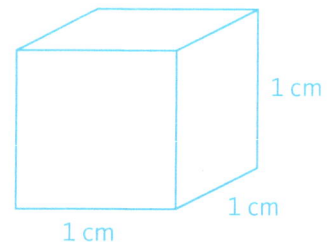

Common Cubic Units	**Metric Cubic Units**
Cubic Inch	Cubic Centimeter
Cubic Foot	Cubic Meter
Cubic Yard	

(See VOLUME)

CUBIC EQUATION

A polynomial equation in which the highest power of an unknown, or variable, is 3.

Example: $5X^3 + 2X^2 + x + 7 = 18$

CUP

A unit of measurement of capacity in the customary measurement system, a cup is equal to 8 fluid ounces. Abbreviation: c

2 c = 1 pint

CURRENCY

Money in any form when used as a medium of exchange.

(See MONEY)

CURVE

A continuous path of points, with the location of the points determined according to conditions that can be specified.

Picture a curve as anything you could draw with a pencil by moving the point without ever lifting it. It doesn't matter whether the path you choose is straight, rounded or has sharp angles because only the most basic feature of a curve is important: that it is a continuous path of points.

As a concept of geometry, the exact definition of a curve can be difficult because our concept of the word leads us to immediately picture an arc or rounded line. But a straight line is considered a curve because it fits the above definition. You can draw a line without lifting your pencil.

To understand the concept of a curve, you must understand the concept of a line. A line is one-dimensional, having only length, and extends to infinity in two directions. It has zero width. If you draw a line with a pencil, the pencil mark has a measurable width, but the pencil line is just a way to illustrate the idea on paper. In geometry a line has no width.

continued ⟶

CURVE CONTINUED

Note that if a curve completely encloses a region of a plane it is a closed curve. Examples include circles, ellipses and polygons. Open curves such as parabolas and spirals have infinite length.

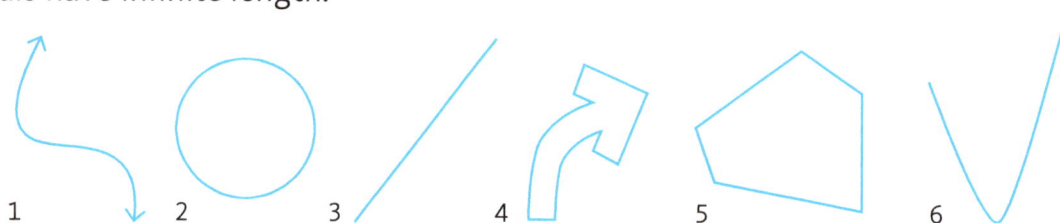

1   2   3   4   5   6

All the above fit the mathematical definition of curves. 2, 4 and 5 are closed curves.

(See LINE, CLOSED CURVE, POINT)

CUSTOMARY SYSTEM OF MEASUREMENT

The system of measurement commonly used in the United States. The customary system includes units for measuring length, weight, capacity, area, volume and temperature.

(See MEASUREMENT)

CYLINDER

A three dimensional figure that has two congruent circular or elliptical bases in parallel planes and a curved surface formed by line segments that join the corresponding points on these bases. If the bases are circles and a line joining the centers of the two bases (the axis) is perpendicular to both planes, it is a right circular cylinder.

Picture a can of soup or a grain silo.

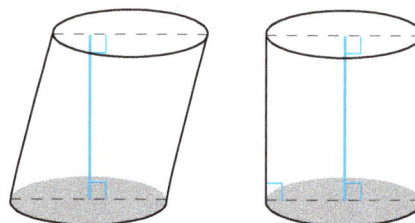

Circular cylinder   Right circular cylinder

A solid object with two identical flat ends that are circular or elliptical and one curved side.

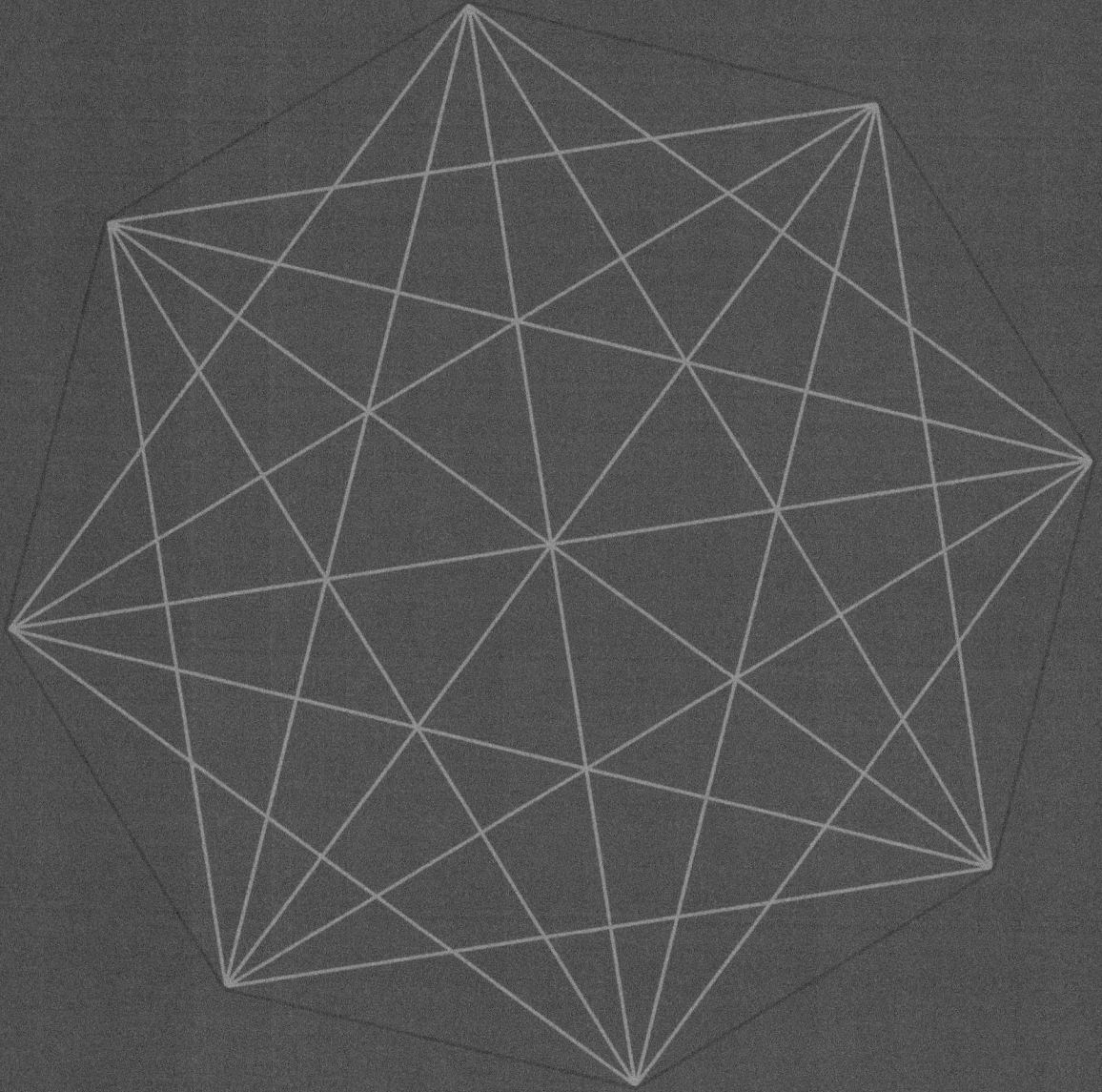

DATA

Facts or information gathered from an experiment, a survey or from observations. Data are often organized and displayed in tables or graphs.

Data is the plural form of the word datum.

(See SURVEY)

DAY

The period of time it takes the Earth to spin once on its axis. We measure a day in 24 hours, from midnight to the next midnight.

DEBIT

Something which is owed and must be deducted at some time. The opposite of credit.

DECA (DEKA)

A prefix that means multiplied by ten. It is derived from the Greek word meaning ten.

Examples:
1 decameter = 10 meters
1 decagram = 10 grams

DECADE

A measure of time, a decade is equal to ten years.

DECAGON

A polygon that has ten sides and ten interior angles. The sum of the interior angles is equal to 1440 degrees.

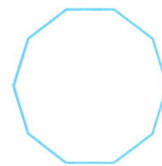

Regular Decagon   Irregular Decagon

DECI-

Prefix that means multiplied by one tenth or $\frac{1}{10}$.

Examples:
1 decimeter = $\frac{1}{10}$ of a liter or 0.1 liter (written dL)
1 decigram = $\frac{1}{10}$ of a gram or 0.1 gram (written dg)

DECIMAL

A number that contains a decimal point (or period) followed by digits to the right of the point. Digits to the right of the decimal point have values less than one.

(See DECIMAL FRACTION, DECIMAL POINT)

DECIMAL FRACTION

A fraction with a denominator (bottom number) of a power of ten:
$(\frac{1}{10}; \frac{1}{100}; \frac{1}{1000}; ...)$.

Decimal fractions are commonly written as numbers following a decimal point.

Examples:

Fractions	$\frac{3}{10}$	$\frac{2}{100}$	$\frac{7}{1000}$
Equivalent decimal fractions	0.3	0.02	0.007

The same fractions expressed as digits following a decimal point.

(See DECIMAL POINT, FRACTION))

DECIMAL NUMBER SYSTEM

A system of numeration based on ten. In the decimal number system, a digit in any place represents ten times what it would represent in the place to its right.

The number system we use is a place value system with a base 10. It is called the decimal number system because it uses ten digits and each place in a number represents a power of ten.

In the base 10 or decimal system the 10 digits are 0, 1, 2, 3, 4, 5, 6, 7, 8, and 9. By using place value, these digits can represent any number. The value of each position within a number is equal to a power of 10. In a number written in base 10 the first position to the left of the decimal represents 1. The second position represents 10. The third position represents 100, or 10 to the second power. The fourth position represents 1000 or 10 to the third power. Thus 3975 in base ten represents:

3 × 1000
9 × 100
7 × 10
5 × 1

millions	hundred thousands	ten thousands	thousands	hundreds	tens	ones	.	tenths	hundredths	
1	0	0	0	0	0	1	.	0	0	or "one million and 1"

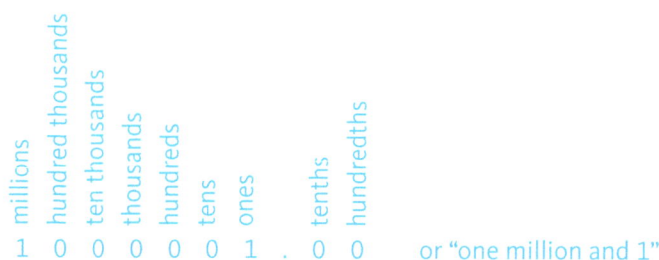

The value of any digit in a number written using the decimal system will depend on its place within the number and will be a power of ten.

(See BASE, PLACE VALUE, POWER)

DECIMAL POINT

A dot or period used to separate a whole number from any fractional part of the number. Places to the right of the decimal point represent fractional parts in this order: tenths, hundredths, thousandths ...

Example: in the number 36.9 the decimal point separates the 36 (the whole number part) from the 9 (the fractional part, which represents 9 tenths or $\frac{9}{10}$).

DECOMPOSE

To break apart. A number can be broken apart to form smaller quantities. In geometry, a figure may be decomposed to form other figures.

Examples: The number 6451 can be decomposed into 6 thousands, 4 hundreds, 5 tens and 1 unit.

A parallelogram can be broken apart to form a trapezoid and a triangle.

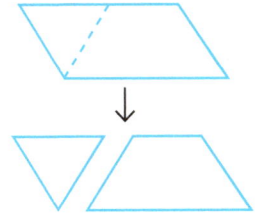

DEDUCT

1) To take away from or subtract.

Example: A store will deduct 10% of the price of an item for valued customers.

2) To reach a conclusion by reasoning.

DEDUCTION

1) A conclusion reached by reasoning.

2) The action of subtracting something.

DEGREE

1) Unit of measure for angles.

To measure angles, we divide a full rotation around a circle into 360 degrees and count one degree as equal to $\frac{1}{360}$. Angles are measured in number of degrees:

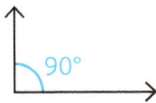

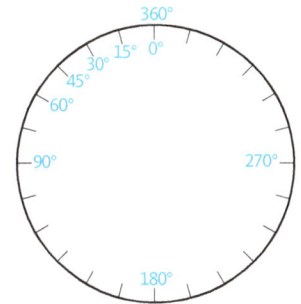

90°

180°

$\frac{1}{4}$ of a rotation is equal to 90° $\frac{1}{2}$ of a rotation is equal to 180°

continued ⟶

DEGREE CONTINUED

2) A unit of measure of temperature. The two most common scales for measuring temperature are Fahrenheit and Celsius.

On the Celsius scale water freezes at 0°C and boils at 100°C.
On the Fahrenheit scale water freezes at 32°F and boils at 212°F.

3) A unit based on a coordinate system of the earth's surface and used to give geographical location. The geographic coordinate system enables every location on the Earth to be specified by a set of numbers or letters called degrees latitude and degrees longitude.

4) In a polynomial, the highest power of a variable that appears in the polynomial.

DEKA-

Prefix that means multiplied by ten. Most frequently spelled deca.

(See DECA)

DENOMINATOR

1) One of the terms in a fraction, the denominator is the number below the fraction bar. The denominator indicates the number of equal parts into which one whole is divided; that is, how many fractional parts there are in the whole.

The word denominator comes from the word nominate or name. It names the number of fractional parts.

Example: In the fraction $\frac{3}{5}$, the denominator (or the 5) indicates that the whole is divided into 5 equal parts. The numerator tells us that we have 3 of them.

2) The denominator is the second term in a ratio.

(See FRACTION, NUMERATOR, RATIO)

DENSITY

A ratio of mass to volume, density is a measure of how much matter is contained in a certain volume. Materials vary greatly in density.

Example: A standard gold bar is quite small to have a mass of 1 kilogram. 1 kilogram of water (at 4°C) is equal to one liter of water. Water is much less dense than gold.

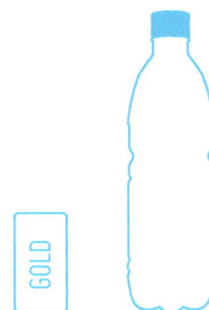

We measure mass by weighing, but weight and mass are not really the same thing.

(*See MASS, VOLUME, WEIGHT*)

DEPENDENT EVENT

Two events are said to be dependent when the outcome of one event changes the probability of the other.

Example: If you are drawing cards from a regular deck of playing cards, drawing one card out at a time and not putting that card back into the deck each time, then the outcome of the first draw affects the outcome of the second. There are fewer cards remaining for the second draw, and the card that you drew on your first turn is not available. The second draw would be a dependent event, as would the third and all subsequent draws.

DEPENDENT VARIABLE

A variable whose value is determined by the value of an independent variable. In a function, the dependent variable is the output of the function and depends on the input or independent variable.

Example: In the function $f(X) = Y$, the value of Y depends on the value you assign to X. Y is a dependent variable.

DESCARTES, RENE

(1596 – 1650) French mathematician. The rectangular coordinate system is named for him.

(*See CARTESIAN COORDINATE SYSTEM*)

DESCENDING ORDER

Arranged from largest to smallest. Decreasing in size.

Example of numbers arranged in descending order: 44, 33, 22, 11

DIAGONAL

1) A line segment that joins any two nonadjacent (not next to each other) vertices of a polygon. The formula for finding the number of diagonals of any polygon is:

$$\text{Number of diagonals} = \frac{(\text{number of sides}) \times (\text{number of sides - 3})}{2}$$

A pentagon has five diagonals

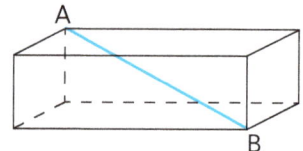

2) A line segment that joins two vertices of a polyhedron that are not in the same face.

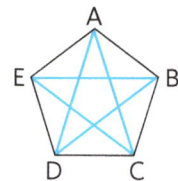

A diagonal of a polyhedron

DIAMETER

1) A line segment that passes through the center of a circle and has endpoints on the circle.

2) A line segment that passes through the center of a sphere and has endpoints on the sphere.

Note: Circles and spheres have an infinite number of diameters all measuring the same.

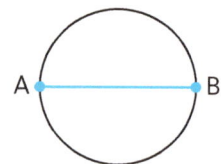

Diameter of a circle

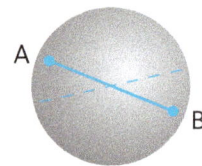

Diameter of a sphere

DIFFERENCE

The result of subtracting two numbers. It is the answer to the question how many more or how many fewer.

Example: In the equation 8 − 3 = 5, 5 is the difference.

If we locate two points on a number line, the distance between them will be the absolute value of their difference.

(See ABSOLUTE VALUE)

DIGIT

A basic symbol used in a numeration system. In the base ten numeration system, we use the ten digits 0, 1, 2, 3, 4, 5, 6, 7, 8, 9.

Some systems of numeration have fewer digits, such as the binary system which only uses two digits, 0 and 1. Some systems of numeration use many more than ten digits, such as the hexadecimal system.

(See DECIMAL NUMBER SYSTEM)

DIHEDRAL ANGLE

An angle formed by the intersection of two planes.

(See ANGLE, PLANE)

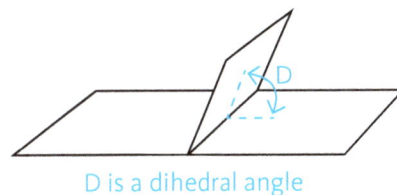

D is a dihedral angle

DIME

A coin whose value is $\frac{1}{10}$ of a U.S. dollar. It is equivalent to 10 cents and written as 10¢ or $0.10.

DIMENSION

A measure of length.

Examples: width, depth and height are dimensions.

A point has no width, depth or height but is only a location. A point has no dimension.

A line has one dimension, it has only length. A line is one dimensional.

Shapes in a plane have two dimensions, or measures of length in two directions, commonly called length and width. (Note that width is just a measure of length in a second direction). A shape in a plane has no depth.

Volumes in space are three dimensional. They have measures of height, width and depth. These are objects in the three dimensional real world.

Examples: A book and your shoes – and you! – are three dimensional.

Note: The dimension identifies the number of coordinates that need to be used to specify a location within the space.

Example: Because a plane has two dimensions, we use a coordinate system with two coordinates (x,y) to position points in a plane. Because a line has only one dimension, we can locate a point on a line using only one letter.

(See CARTESIAN COORDINATE SYSTEM)

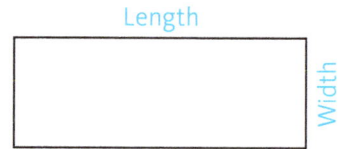

Length
Line

Length

Width

Plane figures have two dimensions, length and width

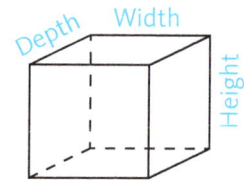

Depth   Width

Height

Three dimensional object

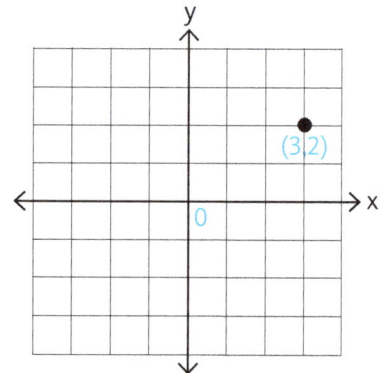

y

(3,2)

0

x

Two dimensional plane

DISJOINT

Two sets are disjoint if they have no members in common.

If the intersection of two sets, set A and set B, is the empty set, the sets A and B are disjoint.

Example: The set of all dogs and the set of all rocks have no common members and are disjoint.

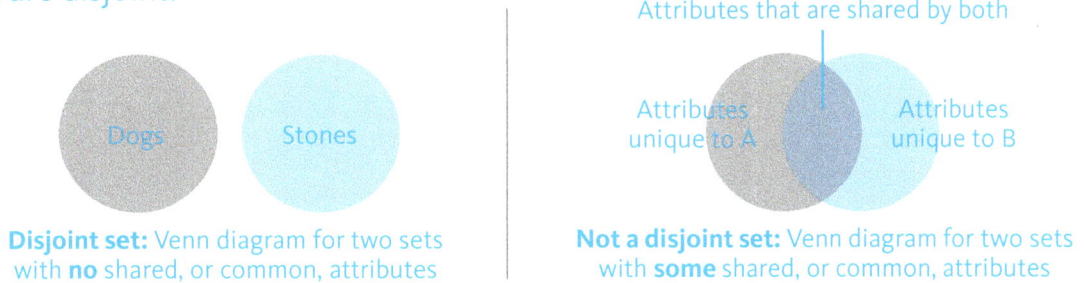

Attributes that are shared by both

Attributes unique to A

Attributes unique to B

Disjoint set: Venn diagram for two sets with **no** shared, or common, attributes

Not a disjoint set: Venn diagram for two sets with **some** shared, or common, attributes

DISTRIBUTIVE PROPERTY

(Sometimes referred to as the distributive law.)

One of the three properties of operations, the distributive property of multiplication over addition states that you get the same result if you multiply a number by a group of numbers that have already been added together, or do each multiplication separately then add the products.

Distributive property of multiplication over addition:
$a \times (b + c) = (a \times b) + (a \times c)$

The distributive property often makes numbers easier to work with because it allows you to multiply a sum by multiplying addends within the sum separately and then adding the products. This allows you to substitute a group of simpler multiplications for one difficult multiplication:

Examples:
$7 \times 7 = 7 \times (5 + 2) = (7 \times 5) + (7 \times 2) = 35 + 14 = 49$

$5 \times 175 = 5 \times (100 + 70 + 5) = 500 + 350 + 25 = 875$

(See ASSOCIATIVE PROPERTY, COMMUTATIVE PROPERTY)

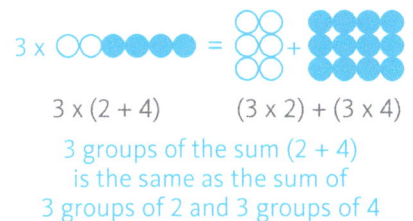

$3 \times (2 + 4)$ $(3 \times 2) + (3 \times 4)$

3 groups of the sum (2 + 4) is the same as the sum of 3 groups of 2 and 3 groups of 4

DIVIDE

To separate into equal parts.

Example: If three friends want to share fifteen pieces of candy, they will divide the candy into three equal parts. Each of the smaller groups will contain five pieces of candy.

$$15 \div 3 = 5$$

DIVIDEND

In division this is the number that is to be separated into equal parts or shares.

Example: In the problem $15 \div 3 = 5$, 15 is the dividend.

DIVISIBLE

One number is divisible by another if there is no remainder after dividing.

Example: Fourteen is divisible by seven because seven divides fourteen into two equal parts with no remainder. $14 \div 7 = 2$

Fifteen is not divisible by seven because seven divides fifteen into two equal parts leaving a remainder of 1.
$15 \div 7 = 2$ with a remainder of 1

(See DIVIDE)

DIVISION

The process of finding how many times one number is contained in another.

One of the basic operations of arithmetic, division separates a quantity into a specified number of equal parts.

Division is the inverse, or opposite, operation of multiplication.
If A × B = C   then   C ÷ A = B

Example: 7 × 2 = 14   so   14 ÷ 7 = 2   and   14 ÷ 2 = 7

Note that the divisor can never be equal to zero because there is no number, A, which, when multiplied by 0, results in B. Zero times any number is equal to zero.

Example: Remember that C ÷ B = A means that A × B = C.
14 ÷ 7 = 2 because 7 × 2 = 14

Now let's try that with 0. 14 divided by 0. It would mean that there is some number, A, such that A times 0 is equal to 14 (14 ÷ 0 = A because A × 0 = 14). But any number multiplied by 0 is equal to zero, so this is impossible.

Let's look at another example of dividing by 0.
If you had 12 cookies, you could divide them into 6 groups of 2.
        12 ÷ 2 = 6
If you had 12 cookies, you could divide them into 4 groups of 3.
        12 ÷ 3 = 4
If you had 12 cookies, you could divide them into 3 groups of 4.
        12 ÷ 4 = 3
If you had 12 cookies, how many groups of 0 would you have?
        12 ÷ 0 = ?

Could you divide the cookies into 5 groups of zero? Twenty groups of zero? A hundred groups of zero? What number times 0 is equal to 12?

(See DIVIDE, INVERSE OPERATION, PARTITIVE DIVISION, QUOTATIVE DIVISION)

DIVISOR

The number you divide by in a division problem. The quantity that specifies the number of parts that the dividend is separated into.

Example: in the problem 15 ÷ 3 = 5, 3 is the divisor.
15 is divided into 3 equal parts of 5 each.

It is important to note that the divisor can never be equal to zero.

(See DIVISION)

DODECAGON

A polygon with twelve sides.

(See POLYGON)

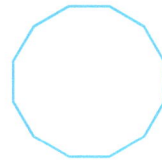

DODECAHEDRON

A three dimensional figure with twelve faces. If each of the faces is a regular pentagon, the dodecahedron is one of the five regular polyhedron.

(See REGULAR POLYHEDRON)

Dodecahedron

DOLLAR

A standard monetary unit of the United States equal to 100 cents. Many other countries use the dollar as the basis for their currency.

(See MONEY)

DOMAIN

All possible values that can be used as input to a function. The set of all possible values for the input number.

(See FUNCTION, MAPPING)

DOUBLE

1) To multiply by 2.

2) An addition fact displayed in addition tables. In doubles, both addends are the same number.

+	1	2	3	4	5	6	7	8	9	10
1	2	3	4	5	6	7	8	9	10	11
2	3	4	5	6	7	8	9	10	11	12
3	4	5	6	7	8	9	10	11	12	13
4	5	6	7	8	9	10	11	12	13	14
5	6	7	8	9	10	11	12	13	14	15
6	7	8	9	10	11	12	13	14	15	16
7	8	9	10	11	12	13	14	15	16	17
8	9	10	11	12	13	14	15	16	17	18
9	10	11	12	13	14	15	16	17	18	19
10	11	12	13	14	15	16	17	18	19	20

Addition table with doubles highlighted

DOZEN

A set of twelve. A group of twelve items.

Example: An egg carton which has 12 compartments will hold a dozen eggs.

DRY MEASURE

Units used to measure the volume of bulk items such as fruits, vegetables or grains. Dry pints and quarts are a little larger than liquid pints and quarts.

1 pint dry = 1.16 pints liquid
1 quart dry = 1.16 quarts liquid
1 peck = 8 dry quarts
4 pecks = 1 bushel

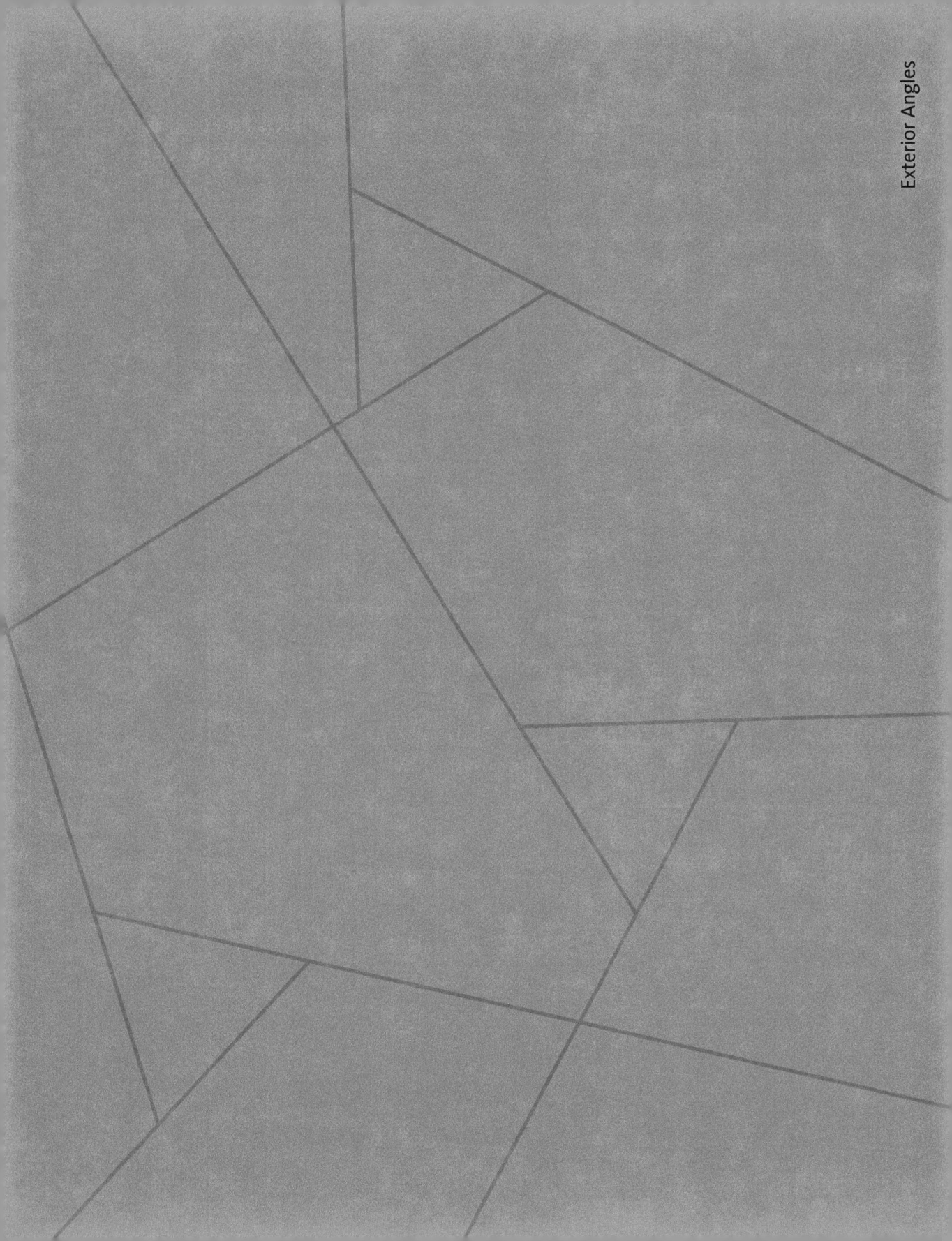

e

Often called Euler's number after 18th century Swiss mathematician Leonhard Euler, the number e is an important number in mathematics. The first few digits are of e are: 2.7182818284590452353602874711....

e is the base of the natural logarithm.

(See LOGARITHM)

EDGE

In a three dimensional figure, the line segment formed where two faces meet.

A cube has 12 edges.

(See POLYHEDRON)

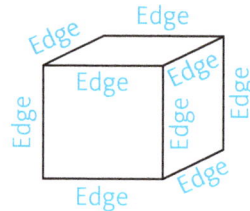

ELAPSED TIME

Period of time during which an event occurs. To find elapsed time you must have a starting time and an ending time.

Example: A train arrived at Grand Central Station at 12:33 p.m. and left the station at 12:38 p.m. Five minutes elapsed while the train was at the station.

ELEMENT

A member of a set.

Example: The set of digits in the base ten is {0, 1, 2, 3, 4, 5, 6, 7, 8, 9}
2 is an element of this set.

ELLIPSE

An ellipse is similar to a circle in that it is a set of points in a plane that form a regular closed curve.

The points on the ellipse are determined by two points within the ellipse called the foci. The distance from one of the foci to a point on the ellipse plus the distance from the other foci to the same point on the ellipse always equals the same number. It is one of the conic sections.

(See CONIC SECTION)

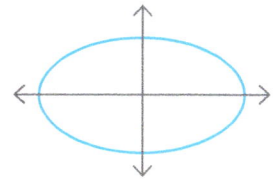

An ellipse has two lines of symmetry

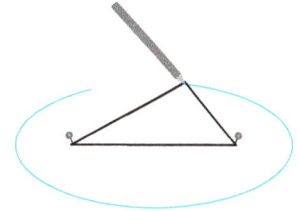

An ellipse can be drawn with string and two fixed points, or foci

ELLIPSOID

A three dimensional figure formed by rotating an ellipse around one of its axes of symmetry.

If you rotate an ellipse around one axis of symmetry and then around its other axis of symmetry, will the resulting ellipsoids be identical?

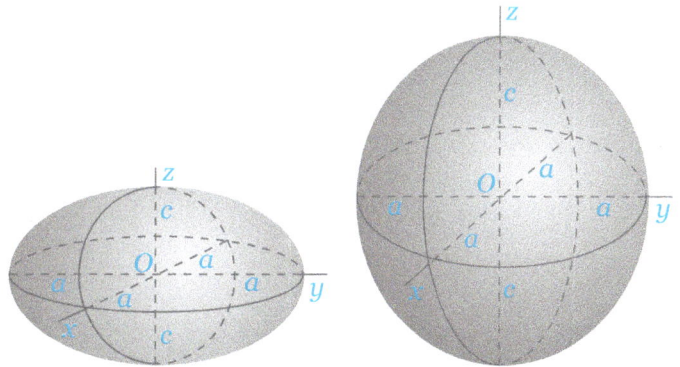

EMPTY SET

A set with no members.

Example: The set of elephants with green spotted fur is an empty set.

ENDPOINT

The point at the end of a line segment or ray. A line segment has two endpoints. A ray has one endpoint.

A ●————————● B
Points A and B are the endpoints of line segment AB.

A ●————————→
Point A is the endpoint of ray AB.

EQUAL

Exactly the same. Having the exact same size, quantity or value.

Examples: Three plus five is equal to eight. (3 + 5 = 8)
The area of a unit square equals one square unit.

EQUAL SIGN

The symbol = . In a number relationship, the equal sign shows that what is written to the left of the sign is equal in value, size or amount to what is written to the right of the sign.

Examples: 3 + 5 = 8
In a rectangular polygon, length × width = area

EQUALITY

The state of being equal. Equality is the relationship between two things that have the same quantity, size or value.

(See EQUAL)

EQUATION

An equation is an expression using mathematical symbols and stating that two things have exactly the same value.

Examples: $3 + 5 = 8$ $7n + 5 = 19$ $7n = 19 - 5$ $7n = 14$ $n = 2$

EQUIANGULAR

Having angles of equal measure. Equiangular polygons are polygons with equal angles. Note that equiangular polygons need not be equilateral.

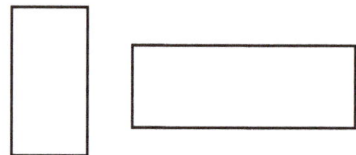

Rectangles are equiangular

EQUIDISTANT

A point in a plane or in space that is the exact same distance from two or more other points.

Example: All the points on a circle are equidistant from the point at its center.

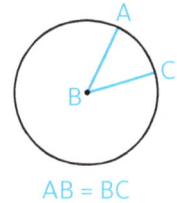

AB = BC

EQUILATERAL

Having all sides of exactly the same length.

An equilateral triangle has three sides of the same length. All angles in an equilateral triangle are also equal and measure 60°.

A square is an equilateral rectangle. Note that not all equilateral quadrilaterals are equiangular.

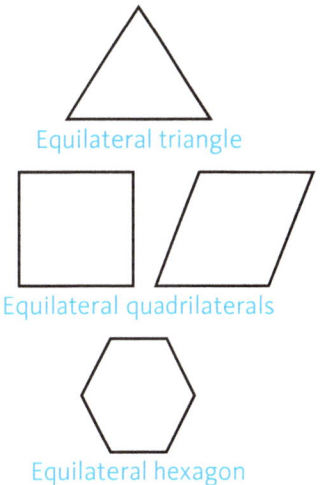

Equilateral triangle

Equilateral quadrilaterals

Equilateral hexagon

EQUIVALENT

Having the same value.

Examples: 212° on the Fahrenheit scale is equivalent to 100° on the Celsius scale. 1 dollar is equivalent to 100 cents.

EQUIVALENT FRACTIONS

Fractions with the same value; fractions that name the same number.

Example: $\frac{2}{4}$, $\frac{3}{6}$, and $\frac{4}{8}$ are all equivalent to $\frac{1}{2}$. They all name the same quantity.

ERATOSTHENES SIEVE

A prime number sieve, this ancient algorithm finds all prime numbers up to any given limit by marking as composite numbers all the multiples of each prime number beginning with the multiples of 2.

ESTIMATE

1) *(noun)* A value close to an exact number that can be used when the exact number is not known or is not needed. An estimate is often calculated from a selected sample.

2) *(verb)* To calculate a value as close as possible to an exact number when the specific number is not needed or is not possible to obtain.

EUCLID

A Greek mathematician who studied in Alexandria during the reign of Ptolemy I (323–283 BC) and who is often called the Father of Geometry. Euclid's Elements is one of the most influential works in the history of mathematics; it focused on developing a logical structure through proofs. In the Elements, Euclid deduced the principles of what we now call Euclidean geometry and wrote works on perspective, conic sections, spherical geometry, and number theory.

EUCLIDEAN GEOMETRY

A specific system of geometry that develops the study of measurement and the relationships of points, lines, angles, and figures in space based on their defining characteristics. Beginning with only a few assumed properties and operating in accordance with a specific set of assumptions, Euclidean Geometry forms a small set of intuitive axioms and from these logically reasons many other theorems.

Euclidean geometry begins with plane geometry, still taught in secondary school as the first axiomatic system and the first examples of formal proof. It goes on to study the geometry of three dimensions.

(See GEOMETRY)

EULER

Leonhard Euler (1707 – 1783). He is considered to be the pre-eminent mathematician of the 18th century, and one of the greatest mathematicians ever to have lived.

Euler is recognized for developing mathematical notation, much of which is still commonly used today. He developed e for the natural logarithm, i for imaginary number, and π for the ratio of the circumference of a circle to its radius.

EVALUATE

Substituting given values for the variables in an algebraic expression or equation and then performing the specified operations.

Example: Evaluate 6a – 2b when a = 12 and b =7.
6a — 2b = 6(12) — 2(7) = 72 – 14 = 48

EVEN NUMBER

Any integer that can be divided by 2 leaving a remainder of 0. Even numbers will end in 2, 4, 6, 8, or 0.

Example: 24 is an even number; 37 is not an even number.

EVENT

Possible outcomes of a probability experiment.

An event is one of a set of outcomes any one of which may or may not occur as a result of an experiment with a random outcome.

Example: If a set of events is given as the probability of the sum on two dice being 5, the set of possible events is {(1, 4) (2, 3) (3, 2) (4, 1)}

EXPANDED NOTATION

Writing a number as a sum of each of its digits multiplied by the digits matching place value. This notation shows the exact value of each digit within the number. Also called expanded form.

Example: the number 3657 written in expanded notation:
$(3 \times 1000) + (6 \times 100) + (5 \times 10) + (7 \times 1)$
or $(3 \times 10^3) + (6 \times 10^2) + (5 \times 10) + (7 \times 1)$

EXPERIMENT

In probability an experiment is an activity that has two or more possible outcomes. Simple experiments would be tossing a coin or rolling dice.

EXPONENT

A number that shows how many times a base number is to be used as a factor in multiplication. The exponent is written as a small number to the right and above the base number.

Exponents are a simple way of writing a repeated multiplication of a number by itself.

In exponential notation 5^2 simply means that the base 5 is used as a factor two times: 5×5.

5^3 means that the base 5 is used as a factor three times: $5 \times 5 \times 5$.
In algebraic notation, X^n means that X is used as a factor n times.

Example: $5^3 = 5 \times 5 \times 5 = 125$

(See BASE, POWER)

EXPONENTIAL NOTATION

A way to express very large or very small numbers using compact forms to facilitate ease of computation; it makes multiplying and dividing very large and very small numbers easier.

Exponential notation is another term for scientific notation.

Example: For the number 839.426 you would write 8.39426×10^2

(See SCIENTIFIC NOTATION)

EXPRESSION

A mathematical phrase that has no equal sign. A mathematical expression will use numbers (digits or quantities such as π or variables such as X) and operators such as + and -. The numbers and operators will be grouped together to show the value of something.

Examples: 4(n + 7)   5x - 3

EXTERIOR ANGLE

1) The angle between a line forming one side of a polygon and a line extended from one of its adjacent sides.

2) The angles formed to the outside two lines if the lines are cut by a third line called a transversal.

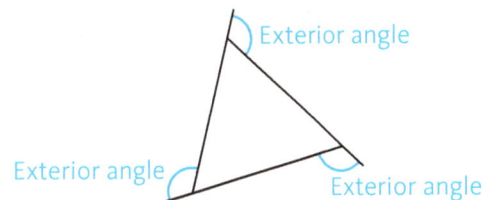

Interior angle

Exterior angle

Exterior angle

Exterior angle

Exterior angle

(See ALTERNATE EXTERIOR ANGLES, INTERIOR ANGLE)

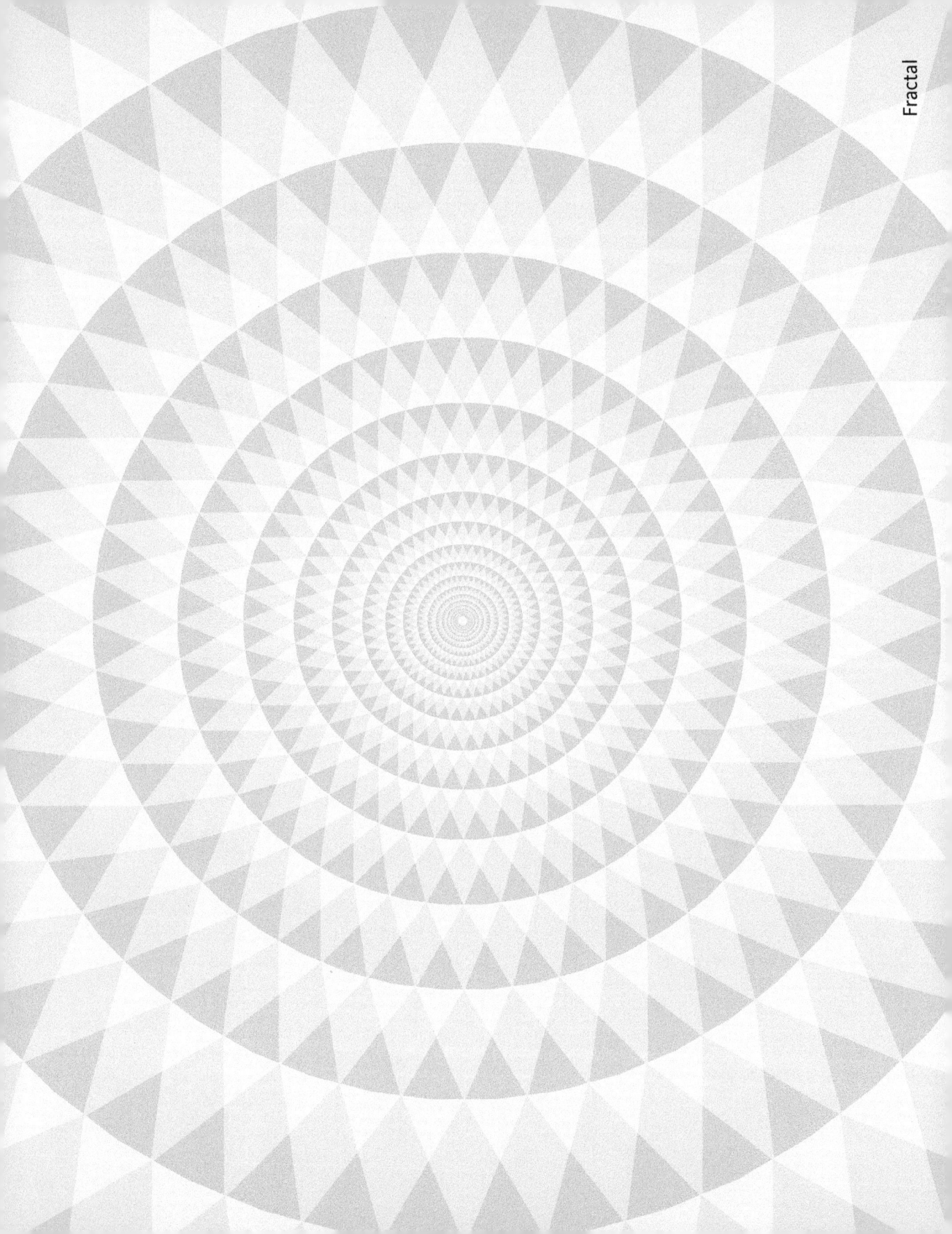

FACE

One of the flat surfaces that form a polyhedron.

A polyhedron is a solid figure bounded by polygons. The polygons that form the surface of any polyhedron are the faces of the polyhedron.

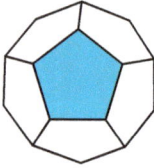

Face of a dodecahedron   Face of a rectangular solid   Face of a square pyramid

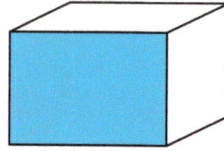

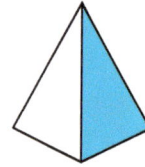

FACT FAMILY

A collection of related addition and subtraction or related multiplication and division basic facts. Fact families are used to help the recall of basic facts.

Example of an addition/subtraction fact family:
$3 + 5 = 8$ $5 + 3 = 8$ $8 - 5 = 3$ $8 - 3 = 5$

Example of a multiplication/division fact family:
$4 \times 3 = 12$ $3 \times 4 = 12$ $12 \div 3 = 4$ $12 \div 4 = 3$

FACTOR

1) *(noun)* The numbers that multiply together to yield a product are its factors.

Example: In the multiplication $3 \times 7 = 21$, 3 and 7 are the factors of the product 21.

Because the inverse of multiplication is division, factors are the numbers that will divide a given quantity leaving no remainder. Any number that divides a quantity and leaves no remainder is a factor of that quantity.

Example: Because 21 can be divided by 3 leaving no remainder, 3 is a factor of 21.
        $21 \div 3 = 7$ remainder 0   3 is a factor of 21.
Because 21 can be divided by 7 leaving no remainder, 7 is a factor of 21.
        $21 \div 7 = 3$ remainder 0   7 is a factor of 21.
So 3 and 7 are factors of 21.

continued ⟶

Note: Many numbers have numerous factors.

The factors of 12 are 1, 2, 3, 4, 6, 12.   2 × 6 = 12, 3 × 4 = 12, 1 × 12 = 12

Some numbers have no factors other than 1 and themselves. The factors of 5 are only 1 and 5. The factors of 13 are only 1 and 13. We call these numbers prime numbers.

2) *(verb)* To find all the factors for a number. When you factor a number, you find all the possible combinations of numbers that when multiplied together result in that number.

Example: Factor 21. *The factors of 21 are 1, 3, 7, and 21.*

(See PRIME FACTORS)

FACTOR PAIR
Any two numbers that when multiplied together, yield a specified product.

Example: The factor pairs for the number 24 are: 1, 24   2, 12   3, 8   4, 6

FACTOR TREE
A diagram used to find the prime factors of a number. Using this method, we continually divide the number by its factors until all the factors remaining are prime numbers. Note: Factor trees are useful in elementary school mathematics when trying to determine the greatest common factor between two numbers.

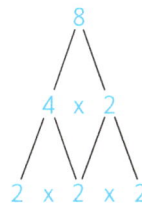

8
4 x 2
2 x 2 x 2

(See FACTOR, GREATEST COMMON FACTOR, PRIME FACTOR)

FACTORIAL

The factorial of a positive integer is the result of multiplying all of the integers from 1 up to and including that integer. We use the sign **!** to indicate a factorial.

Example: $5! = 5 \times 4 \times 3 \times 2 \times 1 = 120$

Note how quickly factorials increase in size.

Examples: $6! = 6 \times 5 \times 4 \times 3 \times 2 \times 1 = 720$ $7! = 7 \times 6 \times 5 \times 4 \times 3 \times 2 \times 1 = 5040$

FACTORING

The process of splitting a mathematical expression into less complicated expressions called its factors.

FAHRENHEIT TEMPERATURE SCALE

A temperature scale based on the one proposed in 1724 by the physicist Daniel Gabriel Fahrenheit, after whom the scale is named.

On the Fahrenheit scale, the freezing point of water is 32 degrees (32°F) and the boiling point of water is 212 degrees (212°F).

By the end of the 20th century, most countries used the Celsius scale rather than the Fahrenheit scale, though the Fahrenheit scale remains the official scale for the United States.

FATHOM

A unit of measure of length, a fathom is equal to 6 feet. Fathoms are used to measure the depth of water.

FIGURATE NUMBERS

Numbers which can be represented as a geometrical shape formed by equally spaced dots. If the arrangement forms a regular polygon, the number is called a polygonal number.

Figurate numbers can also form three-dimensional solids such as a cube.

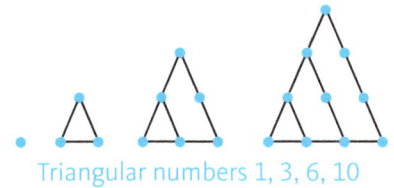
Triangular numbers 1, 3, 6, 10

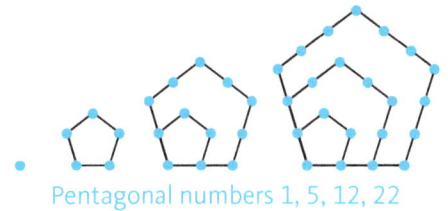
Pentagonal numbers 1, 5, 12, 22

FIBONACCI SEQUENCE

A sequence in which each number equals the sum of the two numbers before it.

The first two Fibonacci numbers are 1, 1 and subsequent numbers in the sequence are the result of adding the two that immediately precede it:
1, 1, 2, 3, 5, 8, 13, 21, 34....

In the natural world we find many instances of mathematical order involving the Fibonacci numbers. Palm trees follow the numbers in the rings on their trunks and many plants follow the Fibonacci numbers in the arrangement of the leaves around the stem.

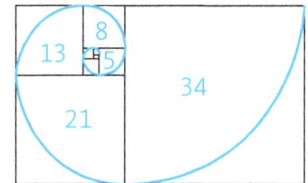

Fitting together squares with the Fibonacci Numbers as widths forms a spiral.

FINITE

When it is possible to measure, count, give a value to or find a limit of something, it is finite.

Note: The opposite of finite is infinite, or something which has no limit.

Examples: The grains of sand on a beach may seem impossible to count, but there is a fixed number of grains at any one time, so there is a finite number of grains of sand.

A line extends in two directions with no end; the length of a line is infinite.

FLAT

A surface containing no points that deviate above or below its plane.

FLIP

A mirror image. Also called a reflection.

(See REFLECTION, REFLECTION SYMMETRY)

FLUID OUNCE

A measure of volume in the customary measurement system.

8 fluid ounces = 1 cup

(See CAPACITY)

FOCAL POINT

Many curves are defined by calculating the distance from a certain point or points to the points that form the curve. For example, an ellipse is formed by all the points that are a constant distance from two central points: the sum of the distances from each of these points is always the same number. A parabola is formed from the set of points equidistant from a given point and a line that doesn't go through that point. In each case, the point or points used to define the curve are called the focal points.

(See CONIC SECTION, ELLIPSE, PARABOLA)

FOOT

A measure of length in the customary measurement system.

1 foot = 12 inches

Note: The plural form of foot is feet.

FORMULA

A mathematical expression used to calculate a specific result, such as the formula to find the area of a rectangle, the formula to find the volume of a sphere or the formula used to convert temperature Celsius to temperature Fahrenheit.

FRACTAL

A never-ending, infinitely complex geometric pattern in which every part, no matter how small, has the same characteristics of the whole. Fractals are created by repeating a simple process over and over again, producing a geometric shape that would still look the same no matter how many times you magnify it because every part repeats. Many fractal patterns appear in nature.

Every part of a fractal is a copy of a larger or smaller part.

FRACTIONS

Numbers that express equal parts of a whole.

A common fraction is a way of expressing a fractional number $\frac{a}{b}$, in which a and b are integers but b is not equal to 0. In common fractions, the bottom number (b), or the denominator, indicates how many equal parts the whole is divided into; the top number, or the numerator (a), indicates how many of these parts you have.

Example: In the common fraction $\frac{3}{4}$, 4 is the denominator and tells us that the whole has been divided into 4 equal parts; 3 is the numerator and tells us that we have 3 of these equal parts.

continued ⟶

FRACTIONS CONTINUED

A fraction is a number, and as such, has a location on the number line.

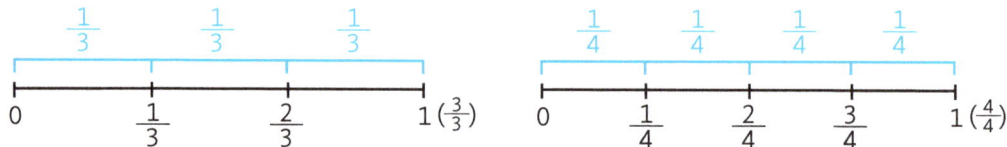

Note: Decimal fractions and percentages are the other methods we use to express fractional parts of numbers.

(See DECIMAL, DENOMINATOR, NUMERATOR, PERCENT, UNIT FRACTION)

FRACTION BAR

The line that separates the numerator and the denominator in a common fraction.

Example: $\frac{22}{7}$

FREQUENCY

1) How many times some event occurs during a specified period of time.

Example: The frequency of a cricket's chirping varies according to temperature.

2) The number of times an item occurs in a set of data.

Example: In a class of 25, 7 students scored A on the math test.

FREQUENCY DISTRIBUTION

An organized display of a set of data that shows how often each different piece of data occurs during each interval. A set of intervals into which the range of a statistical set of data is divided.

(See FREQUENCY, FREQUENCY TABLE)

FREQUENCY TABLE

A table that lists items in a set of data and indicates the number of times each item occurs. A frequency table is often constructed by arranging collected data items randomly and using tally marks to count frequency.

Favorite Food	Tally	Frequency
Taco	卌 ‖	7
Burger	卌 ‖‖	9

Some frequency tables list items in ascending order of magnitude and give their corresponding frequencies.

Grade	Frequency
80-90 (B)	14
70-80 (C)	11
91-95 (A)	5
96-100 (A+)	1

(See FREQUENCY DISTRIBUTION, TALLY CHART)

FUNCTION

A rule that defines a relationship between two sets of numbers or other objects in which each member of a first set is paired with only one member of the second set. The first set is referred to as the domain and the second set is the range.

Each of a function's input values (a value from the domain) gives back exactly one output value (a value in the range).

Example: The function that relates each counting number n to its square n^2

Functions are commonly written as "f(x)" where x is the input value.

Example: f(x) = 5x   (read f of x is 5 multiplied by x)
This is a function, because for every input value of x there is a corresponding output value for f(x):
f(1) = 5   f(2) = 10   f(-5) = -25

(See MAPPING)

FURLONG

A unit of measurement of length, a furlong is equal to 1/8 of a mile. Furlongs are frequently used to measure the distance of horse races.

GALILEO GALILEI

(1564-1642) Italian mathematician and physicist who established the method of studying dynamics by a combination of theory followed by experiment.

GALLON

A unit of measurement of capacity in the customary system.

1 gallon = 4 quarts

(See CAPACITY)

GAME

A mathematical representation of a conflict in which the outcome depends on the choices made by the opponents. The rules, strategies, and outcomes of a game are defined by clear mathematical parameters.

GAUSS, CARL FRIEDRICH

(1777-1855) German mathematician and physical scientist who made significant contributions to many fields: number theory; algebra; statistics; analysis; differential geometry; geophysics; electrostatics; astronomy; optics and more. Considered by many to be greatest mathematician of all time.

GEOBOARD

A mathematical manipulative used to explore the basic concepts of plane geometry such as perimeter, area and the characteristics of polygons.

A geoboard is a rigid board containing either a lattice or a circular pattern of exposed nails; rubber bands are wrapped around the nails to form geometric shapes.

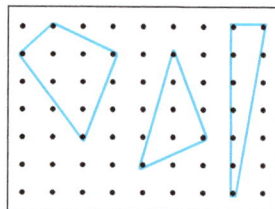

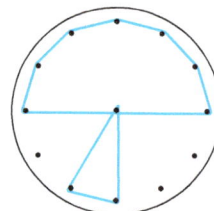

GEODESIC

The geometry of curved surfaces, in which geodesic lines, which are lines on the curved surface, take the place of the straight lines of plane geometry.

GEODESICS

Lines on a surface that curve only to stay on that surface. They are the shortest distance between two points on the curved surface.

Example: If an ant on the surface of a huge ball followed a straight path between two points on the surface, it would perceive its path to be a straight line. The line, though, actually curves with the surface.

GEOMETRIC SEQUENCE

A sequence created by multiplying each consecutive number by a constant value.

In a geometric sequence with the first term **a** and the constant multiplier **r**, the terms of the sequence would be: a, a × r, (a × r) × r (or ar^2), (a × r × r) × r (or ar^3)... ∞. Note that the ratio between any consecutive terms of the sequence is the constant, **r**.

Examples: In the geometric sequence 1, 3, 9, 27..., each number is multiplied by 3 to get the next number. Each number in the sequence is 3 times bigger than the number before it.

In the sequence 3, 6, 12, 24, 48..., each number is 2 times the number before it or 3, 3 × 2, 3 × 4, 3 × 8, 3 × 16...

(See SEQUENCE)

GEOMETRY

The branch of mathematics that studies the properties of points, curves, planes and surfaces in space, and the figures bounded by them.

Plane geometry studies shapes in a plane (flat shapes), such as polygons and other closed curves. Solid geometry studies 3-dimensional (solid) shapes, such as cubes and spheres.

From the Standards: Although there are many different geometries, CCSS mathematics is devoted primarily to plane Euclidean geometry, studied both synthetically (without coordinates) and analytically (with coordinates).

(See CURVE, DIMENSION, EUCLIDEAN GEOMETRY, LINE, PLANE GEOMETRY, POINT)

GIGA

A prefix in the metric system denoting a factor of a billion (10^9 or 1,000,000,000). It has the symbol G.

GOLDEN RATIO

The number [$\frac{(1 + \sqrt{5})}{2}$] or approximately 1.618033989.

This ratio achieves the following:

If you divide a line segment in such a way that the ratio of the entire length of the line to the longer part of the line is equal to the ratio of the longer part of the line to the shorter part, you will have the golden ratio.

To state this another way: If you divide any line into two parts in such a way that the quotient of the entire length divided by the longer part is equal to the quotient of the longer part divided by the smaller part you will have the Golden Ratio.

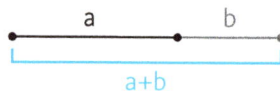

The ratio (a + b) to 'a', equals the ratio 'a' to 'b':
$$\frac{(a+b)}{a} = \frac{a}{b} = 1.618$$

continued $\longrightarrow$

The golden ratio is found often in art and architecture. It was named the golden ratio by the Greeks who used it in their architecture, often when building temples, but the Greeks were not the first to use this proportion in building. An even earlier example of the use of the golden ratio is in the proportions of the Great Pyramid of Giza, believed to be 4,600 years old.

(See RATIO)

GOLDEN RECTANGLE

Throughout history, the ratio for length to width of rectangles of 1.618... has been considered most pleasing to the eye.

A feature of this rectangle is that if a square section is removed, the remaining rectangle is another rectangle with the same ratio as the first. A second square can be removed from this golden rectangle and the remaining rectangle is another rectangle with the same ratio. Squares can be removed repeatedly. When this is done, corresponding corners of the squares that are removed form an infinite sequence of points on the golden spiral.

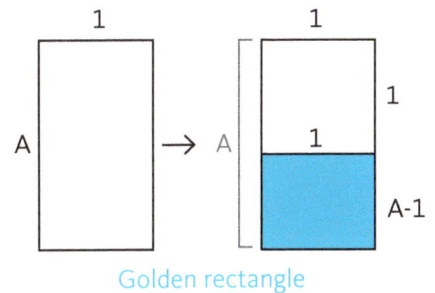

Golden rectangle

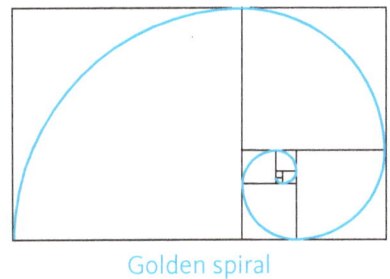

Golden spiral

GOOGOL

The number 10 raised to the power of 100 (10^{100}); written out, this numeral would be the digit 1 followed by 100 zeros.

GRADIENT

The degree of inclination of a straight line.

The gradient will tell you how steep a straight line will appear on a rectangular Cartesian coordinate graph where the gradient is the rate at which the y-coordinate changes with respect to the x-coordinate. Because a gradient has both magnitude and direction, it is a vector quantity.

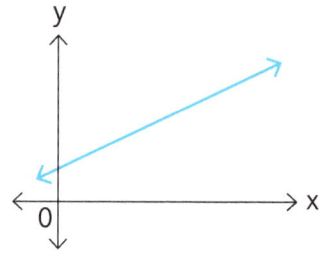

GRAM

A unit of measure of mass (weight) in the metric scale. Abbreviated g.

1,000 grams = 1 kilogram
100 g = 3.5274 oz.

GRAPH

1) A diagram that displays a relationship between two sets of numbers. A set of points on the diagram will have their position determined by the relationship between the numbers.

This graph displays the relation between the month and the average temperature during that month.

2) A diagram of values such as a pie chart or a bar graph used to illustrate relationships between quantities.

Example: A circle graph is a graph in the form of a circle that is divided into sectors, with each sector representing a defined percentage of a set of data.

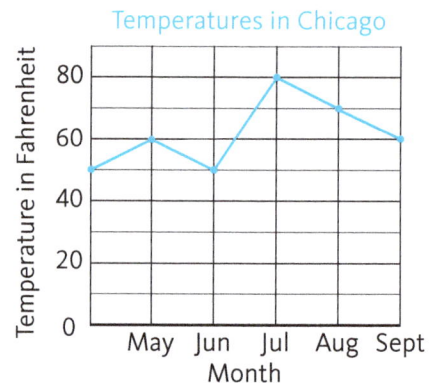

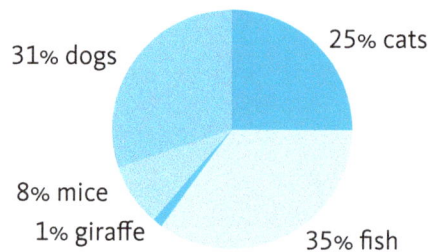

Temperatures in Chicago

A circle graph displaying the different pets of students in our class

continued ⟶

98

3) In algebra, a graph charts the relations between certain quantities when plotted with reference to a set of axes.

Example: All the points with coordinates that satisfy a given equation can be graphed on Cartesian coordinates (an x, y axis) as the positions of points in a plane. This graph will be a line or curve drawn on the coordinate plane by joining the points that represent the ordered pairs that satisfy the equation.

Example: The points on a circle with its center at the origin all satisfy the equation $x^2 + y^2 = r^2$ where r is the radius. When graphed on a coordinate plane, the points that fit the equation can be joined to form the circle.

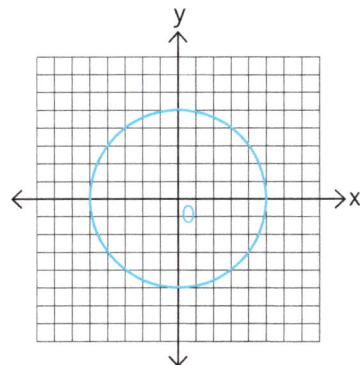

The graph of all points that satisfy the equation $x^2 + y^2 = 25$.

(See BAR GRAPH, CARTESIAN COORDINATES, CIRCLE GRAPH)

GREATER THAN >
The phrase and symbol used to compare two numbers when the first is larger than the second.

Example: 8 > 3 (read eight is greater than three). Note that eight is farther to the right of zero on the number line.

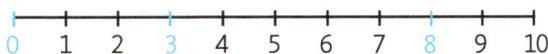

GREATER THAN OR EQUAL TO ≥
Phrase and symbol used to compare two numbers when the first is larger than or equal to the second.

Example: a ≥ 0 (read a is greater than or equal to 0).

GREATEST COMMON FACTOR

The largest number that divides two or more numbers exactly leaving no remainder.

Example: 6 is the greatest common factor of 12 and 30.
The factors of 12 are 1, 2, 3, 4, 6 and 12.
The factors of 30 are 1, 2, 3, 5, 6, 10 and 15.
The greatest factor that they share is 6.

(See COMMON DIVISOR, COMMON FACTOR)

GRID

A set of uniformly spaced horizontal and vertical lines. Because the lines on a grid are spaced at regular intervals, they form squares or rectangles.

This grid of horizontal and perpendicular lines, uniformly spaced, can be used to graph points.

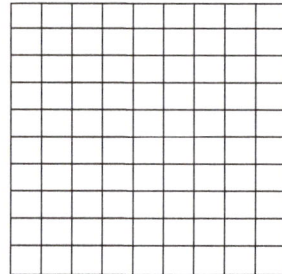

GROSS

1) A set containing twelve dozen. A group of one hundred forty four items.

gross = twelve dozen = 144

2) The total before any deductions.

Example: The gross income from the sale was $200, but after we deducted the cost of supplies we had only $120.

HALF

The fraction that represents one of two equal parts of a whole.

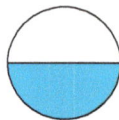

$\frac{1}{2}$ one-half

HALF DOLLAR

A coin with the value of one-half of a U.S. dollar. It is worth 50 cents and is written as 50¢ or $0.50.

HALF HOUR

A unit of measurement for time that is equivalent to thirty minutes.

HALF PAST

Thirty minutes after an hour.

Example: Half past 7 means 30 minutes after 7 or 7:30 (seven thirty).

HECT-

A prefix denoting 100. Hect or hecto is used in the metric system of measurement.

1 hectometer = 100 meters
1 hectogram = 100 grams
1 hectoliter = 100 liters

HEIGHT

The vertical measurement from top to bottom.

In mathematics terms, the 'height' of a geometric figure is properly its altitude and the position of the altitude will vary.

(See ALTITUDE)

HELIX

A three-dimensional curve that lies on a cylinder or a cone, so that its angle to a plane perpendicular to the axis of the cylinder or cone remains constant.

Example: The curve on a screw is a helix.

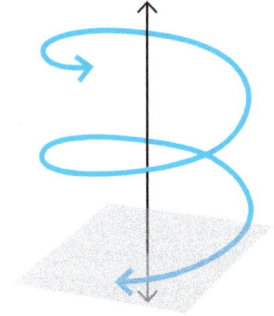

HEMISPHERE

One half of a sphere.

Hemisphere also refers to one half of the Earth.

If the Earth is bisected (cut into two equal parts) at the equator, it is divided into the Northern Hemisphere, or the part of the Earth north of the equator, and the Southern Hemisphere, or the part of the Earth south of the equator.

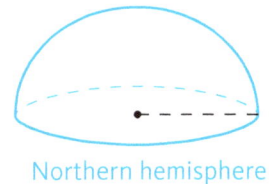

Northern hemisphere

If the Earth is bisected (cut into two equal parts) at a line that runs from pole to pole through Greenwich, England, it is divided into the Western Hemisphere and the Eastern Hemisphere. The half of the Earth west of a line running from the North Pole to the South Pole includes America.

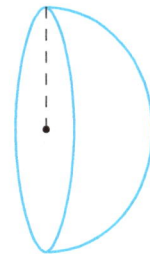

Eastern hemisphere

HENDECAGON

A polygon with 11 sides.

(See POLYGON)

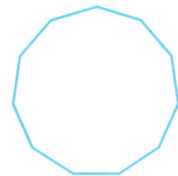

HEPTA-

A prefix meaning 7.

HEPTAGON

A polygon with 7 sides.

(See POLYGON)

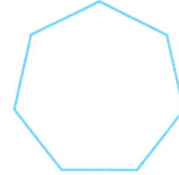

HEXA-

A prefix meaning 6.

HEXAGON

A polygon with 6 sides.

The sum of the angles in a hexagon is 720°.

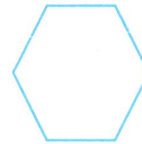 

Hexagon   Concave hexagon

HEXADECIMAL

A place value numeration system using a base of 16.

Because the hexadecimal system uses a base of 16, there are 16 different digits, and any place can show 16 different values instead of only the 10 we are accustomed to in the base 10.

In the hexadecimal system, the digits 0 through 9 are used and then the symbol A is used to represent 10, B to represent 11, C to represent 12, D to represent 13, E to represent 14 and F to represent 15.

Example: The number A4B5 = $(10 \times 16^3) + (4 \times 16^2) + (11 \times 16) + 5 = 42{,}165$

(See BASE)

HEXAHEDRON

A polyhedron with six faces.

A cube is one example of a hexahedron.

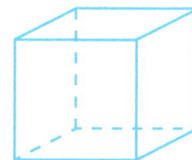

HINDU-ARABIC

Another name for the place value number system that uses the base 10. The base ten system uses the digits 0, 1, 2, 3, 4, 5, 6, 7, 8 and 9 and each place in a number has a value of a power of 10.

Developed between the 1st and 4th centuries by Indian mathematicians, it was adopted by the Persian mathematician Al-Khwarizmi. Use of the system spread to the western world by the Middle Ages.

(See DECIMAL NUMBER SYSTEM)

HISTOGRAM

A graph in which data is grouped into specified ranges and the ranges are plotted as continuous bars of differing heights. Just as with the data in a bar graph, a higher bar indicates a higher frequency of the data within the range; a lower bar indicates a lower frequency of data within the range. The difference between a histogram and a bar graph is that a bar graph organizes data into categories, while a histogram organizes data into intervals.

Because histograms display data that is continuous across the spectrum, the bars in a histogram must be displayed in the order that the data occur. The data displayed flows across the graph and creates a picture of the data distribution.

Example: My new kitty Coco's weight gain from birth through week 7.

Note: The bars of a histogram are connected to show that the data is continuous.

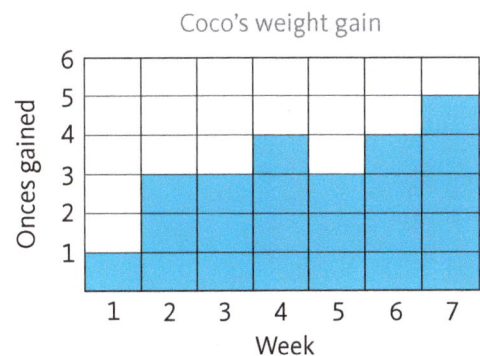

Coco's weight gain

(See BAR GRAPH)

HORIZONTAL

Parallel to or in the plane of the horizon.

In mathematics, a horizontal line is parallel to the x axis in the coordinate plane. The line has no incline: it does not rise or fall at all. When a line is horizontal, all the points on the line have the same y-coordinate.

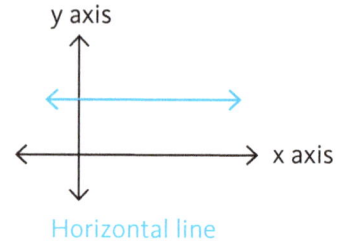

y axis

x axis

Horizontal line

(See CARTESIAN COORDINATE SYSTEM, COORDINATES, ORDERED PAIR)

HORIZONTAL AXIS

(See AXIS definition 2)

HOUR

A unit of measure for time. A day is divided into 24 hours so an hour is $\frac{1}{24}$ of a day. Hour is used in both the common and the metric system and is abbreviated as hr.

1 hour = 60 minutes

HUNDRED

100, a number equal to 10 × 10 or 10^2.

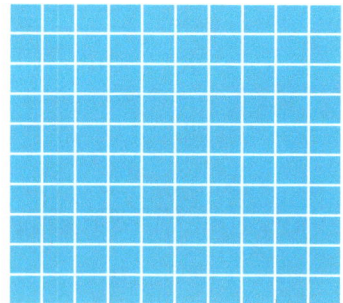

A grid of 100 squares

HUNDREDTH

One of one hundred equal parts of a group or unit. One hundredth is one of the parts that result from dividing something into one hundred equal parts. Hundredths are in the second position to the right of the decimal point in the decimal number system.

One hundredth is written as the fraction $\frac{1}{100}$ or in decimal notation as 0.01.

Examples: 7.02 is read as 7 and 2 hundredths. In the number 46.37, 7 is in the hundredths place.

1 cent is equal to $\frac{1}{100}$ of one dollar.

(See DECIMAL FRACTION, DECIMAL NUMBER SYSTEM)

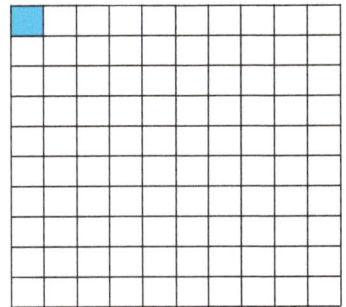

$\frac{1}{100}$ is highlighted

HYPERBOLA

A curve in a plane that has two identical branches. The branches are mirror images of each other. A hyperbola is formed by a set of all points for which the difference of the distances from two fixed points is constant.

A hyperbola is one of the conic sections.

A hyperbola is formed when a plane intersects both halves of a right circular cone at an angle parallel to the axis of the cone.

Example: In this image you can see the two branches of a hyperbola in a plane.

(See CONIC SECTION)

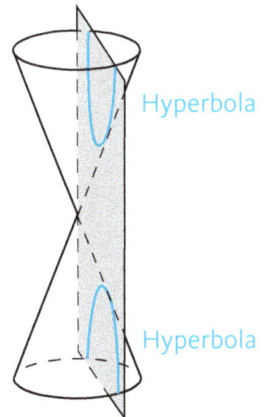

Hyperbola

Hyperbola

HYPOTENUSE

In a right triangle, the side opposite the right angle is called the hypotenuse.

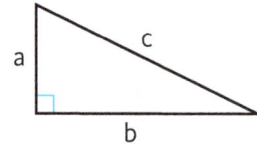

HYPOTHESIS

A statement that attempts to explain something but that has not yet been tested or proved to be correct. A hypothesis might be true or false, and must be tested through careful experimentation or observation.

ICOSAHEDRON

A three dimensional figure that has 20 faces and 30 edges. In a regular icosahedron each face is an equilateral triangle. A regular icosahedron is one of the Platonic Solids.

Icosahedron is taken from Greek icosa- which means 20.

(See PLATONIC SOLIDS, POLYHEDRON, REGULAR POLYHEDRON)

A regular icosahedron

INDEPENDENT VARIABLE

The input of a function. The value of the independent variable is assigned. The dependent variable, or the output of the function depends on the value assigned to the independent variable.

Example: In the equation 3X = Y, if the value of X is given as 7, then the value of Y (the dependent variable) is 21.

(See DEPENDENT VARIABLE)

IDENTITY ELEMENT

A number that, when used with another number in an arithmetic operation, leaves that number unchanged. The identity element in an operation returns any input unchanged.

Examples: The identity element for addition is 0 because 0 + n = n, for any number n. 0 + 8 = 8

The identity element for multiplication is 1 because, for any number n, 1 × n = n. 9 × 1 = 9

IMPROPER FRACTION

A common fraction with a value greater than or equal to 1. An improper fraction has a numerator equal to or greater than its denominator.

Examples: $\frac{5}{3} = 1\frac{2}{3}$ $\frac{4}{4} = 1$

(See COMMON FRACTION, DENOMINATOR, NUMERATOR)

IMAGINARY NUMBER (i)

A number we use to make it possible to solve equations that have no solution within the set of real numbers. The 'unit imaginary number' is the square root of negative 1, or the number that, when multiplied by itself, results in a negative 1. There is no such number in the set of real numbers, so in order to solve these equations, we imagine that there is.

Example: $n^2 = -4$ has no solution in the set of real numbers because the multiplication of two positive numbers or two negative numbers always results in a **positive** number. If we multiply any number, positive or negative, by itself, the result is always positive; so no matter what number n represents, n^2 (n × n) will always be positive.

(See REAL NUMBERS)

INCENTER

In a triangle, the center point of the circle inscribed inside the triangle. The incenter is also the meeting point of the three bisectors of the angles of the triangle.

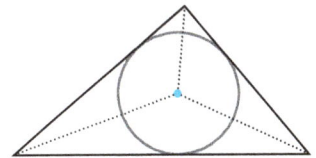

INCH

A unit of measure for length in the common measurement system. Inch is abbreviated in.

12 inches = 1 foot
1 in = 2.54 cm

INCREASE

To enlarge in size or quantity.

INDEPENDENT EVENT

Two events are said to be independent when the outcome of one event does not change the probability of the outcome of the other.

Example: If you a draw card from a regular deck of playing cards and then put that card back into the deck, the outcome of the first draw will not effect the outcome of a second in any way. Because you return any card drawn back into the deck, there will be the same number of cards remaining for the second draw, and the card that you drew on your first turn is still available. The second draw is an independent event; its result is not altered in any way by the first draw.

If you are drawing cards from a regular deck of playing cards and not replacing the cards, the deck changes after every draw. This changes each successive draw and makes them dependent events.

INEQUALITY ≠

A statement that shows that one quantity is not equal to another.

Examples: a ≠ b says that a is not equal to b   9 ÷ 3 ≠ 2 because 9 ÷ 3 = 3

There are other mathematical symbols that show quantities are not equal.

a < b says that a is less than b   2 < 9 ÷ 3
a > b says that a is greater than b   9 ÷ 3 > 2

INFINITE ∞

Unending; without an end or a limit. Infinite is the opposite of finite.

Examples: The set of counting numbers is infinite: 1, 2, 3, 4, 5, 6, 7, 8, 9, 10, 11....

A line extends in two directions to infinity ∞.

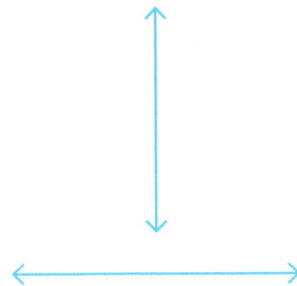

INSCRIBED

To place inside touching as many points as possible.

An inscribed polygon is placed within a circle so that each vertex of the polygon is on the circle.

An inscribed circle is a circle placed within a polygon so that each side of the polygon is tangent to the circle.

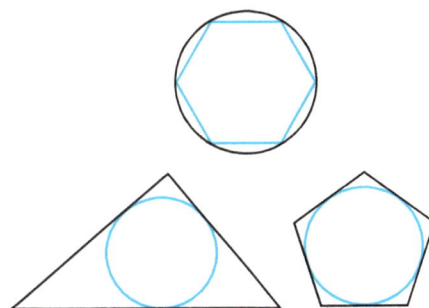

(See INCIRCLE)

INTEGERS

The set of numbers that contains the counting numbers, the negatives of the counting numbers and 0. An integer is a real number that does not contain a fractional part.

-5 -4 -3 -2 -1 0 1 2 3 4 5

The set of integers is infinite in two directions.
It is the set of the counting numbers, their opposites and 0.

INTEREST

A charge made for borrowing money. Interest is paid to the lender of money as a fee for the use of that money.

Examples: Mike borrowed money from the bank to buy a new car. The bank charged him 3% interest on the loan.

Mary had a savings account at the bank. The bank paid Mary 2% interest on the account as a fee for her allowing them to use her money to make other loans.

(See COMPOUND INTEREST)

INTERIOR ANGLE

1) An angle formed inside a polygon by two adjacent sides. A polygon is a surface on a plane enclosed by straight lines and has an interior (inside) and exterior (outside). The interior angles of a polygon are all the angles inside the perimeter formed by any two adjacent sides of the polygon.

2) Angles formed between two straight lines intersected by a third straight line called the transversal. The pairs of angles on opposite sides of the transversal but inside the two lines are called alternate interior angles.

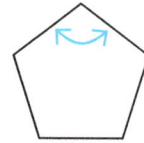

One interior angle of a pentagon

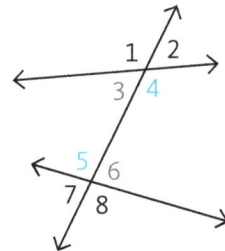

3, 4, 5 and 6 are interior angles.
3 and 6 are alternate interior angles.
4 and 5 are also alternate interior angles.

INTERQUARTILE RANGE

The spread of the middle fifty percent of a set of data. It is the data between the lower and upper quartiles of the set.

The interquartile range, written as IQR, is shown on a box plot.

(See BOX PLOT)

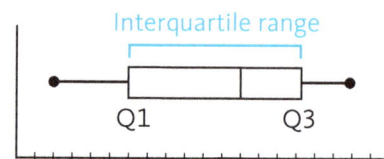

Interquartile range

Q1   Q3

INTERSECT

To meet or cross. To have a point or points in common.

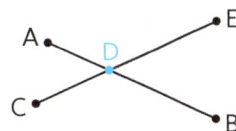

Line segments $\overline{AB}$ and $\overline{CE}$ intersect at point D

1) Lines, line segments and rays intersect at a common point.

2) Planes intersect in a straight line.

3) Sets intersect if they share common elements.

(See INTERSECTION OF SETS)

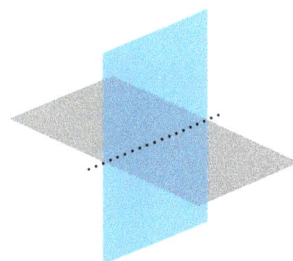

Intersecting planes

INTERSECTION OF SETS

For two sets, set A and set B, a set consisting of all elements that are contained in both A and B is the intersection of these sets.

Example: If set A is the set of all even numbers {2, 4, 6, 8, 10, 12…} and set B is the set of all multiples of 3 {3, 6, 9, 12…}, then the intersection of sets A and B is the set of all numbers contained in both: {6, 12, 18…}

(See SET)

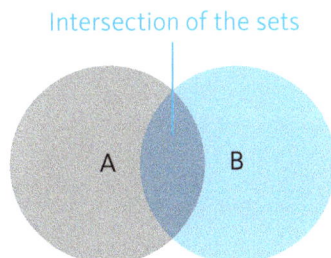

Intersection of the sets

INVERSE OPERATION

An operation that does the exact opposite of another. Inverse operations 'undo' each other's effect.

Examples: Subtraction is the inverse operation of addition. The inverse of adding 3 is subtracting 3.

$5 + 3 = 8$ $8 - 3 = 5$

Division is the inverse operation of multiplication.

The inverse of multiplying by 4 is dividing by 4.

$6 \times 4 = 24$ $24 \div 4 = 6$

IRRATIONAL NUMBER

A real number that cannot be written as a simple fraction. When an irrational number is written as a decimal, the numbers to the right of the decimal point continue to infinity without forming a pattern that repeats.

Examples: The square root of 3 is 1.73205080...
The number π is 3.14159...

Note: Because these numbers cannot be expressed as a common fraction or the ratio of two numbers, they are called irrational.

IRREGULAR POLYGON

A polygon that does not have all sides equal and all angles equal.

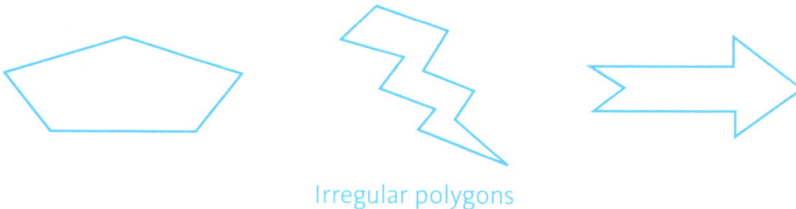

Irregular polygons

ISOMETRY

A transformation in which the original figure and its image are congruent.

(See TRANSFORMATION)

ISOSCELES TRAPEZOID

A trapezoid having non parallel sides of equal length.

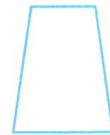

Isosceles trapezoid

ISOSCELES TRIANGLE

A triangle with two sides of equal length. Isosceles traingles also have two equal angles.

Isosceles triangles

ITERATION

Repetition. A computation in which an operation or a series of operations is repeated a number of times.

Example: Prime factorization using factor trees is an iterative process:
$18 = 2 \times 9 = 2 \times 3 \times 3$

JUMP STRATEGY

A method of completing an arithmetic operation by moving along the number line in increments of the numbers involved.

Example: Jumping by parts of a number often makes solving a calculation easier. To add 53 + 44: begin at 53, jump 10, 10, 10, 10 and then 1, 1, 1, 1.

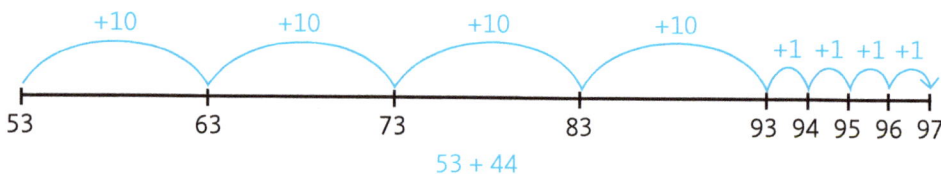

53 + 44

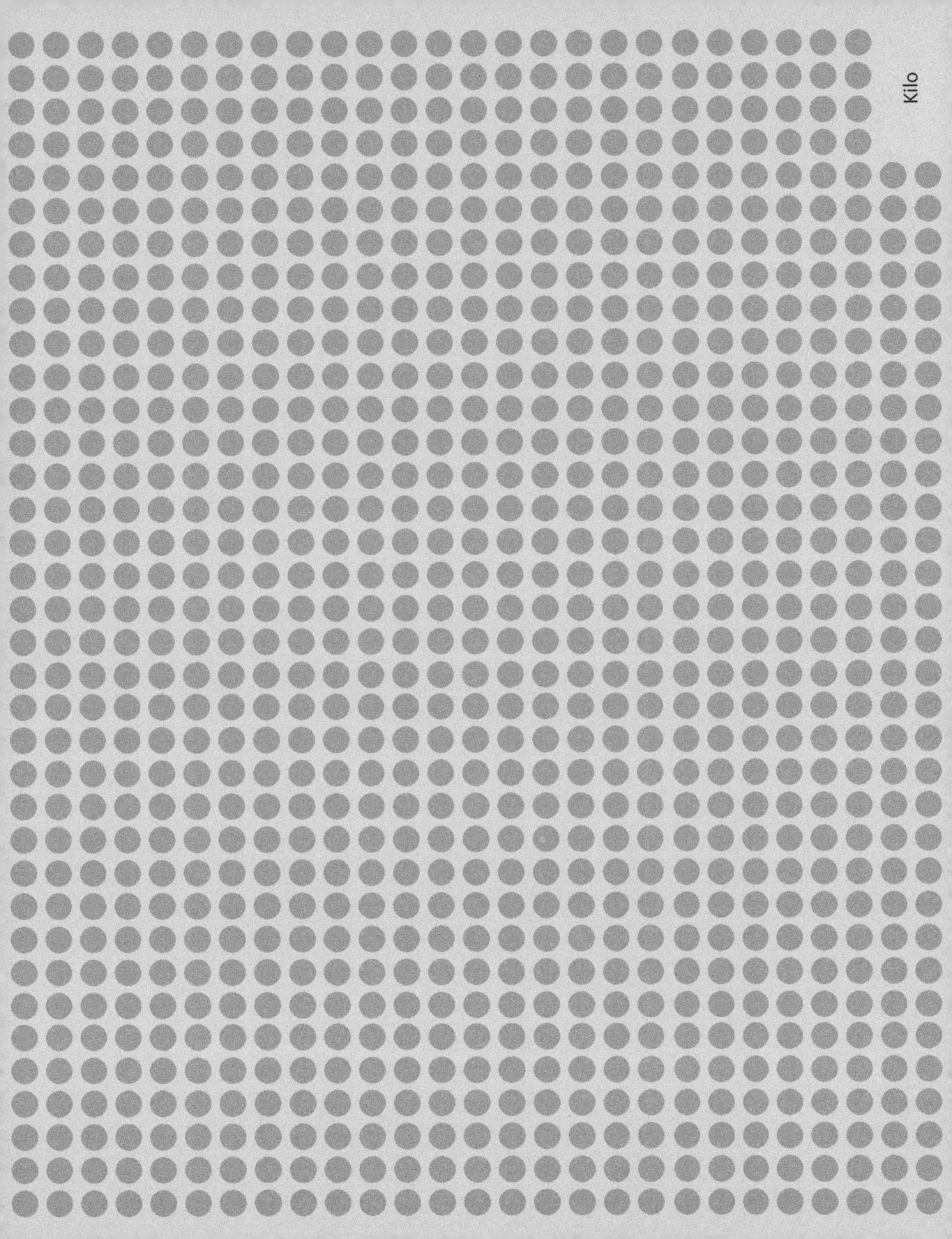

KEY

An explanation of the symbols used in a graph, a chart or a map.

In this example, the key is that each triangle represents 2 slices of pizza.

Number of pizza slices eaten

Suzie	△
Jonathan	△ △
Max	△ △ △
Dora	△
Anthony	△ △

Each △ represents 2 slices of pizza

KELVIN SCALE

A scale for the measurement of temperature with zero set at absolute zero. Absolute zero is a temperature at which there is a complete absence of any heat energy. Temperatures on this scale are called kelvins and not degrees kelvin.

The boiling point of water is 373.15 on the Kelvin scale.

(See CELSIUS, DEGREE, FAHRENHEIT)

KILO-

A prefix in the metric system of measurement that means 1000.

1 kilogram = 1000 grams
1 kilometer = 1000 meters
1 kiloliter = 1000 liters

KILOGRAM

A measure of mass in the metric measurement system. Abbreviation: kg

1 kg = 1,000 grams
1 kg is approximately 2.2 pounds.

KILOLITER

A measure of capacity in the metric measurement system. Abbreviation: kl

1 kl = 1,000 liters
A cube with edges that measure 1 meter has a capacity of 1 kiloliter. One kiloliter of water weighs 1 metric ton.

KILOMETER

A measure of length in the metric measurement system. Abbreviation: km

1 km = 1,000 meters
1 km is approximately 0.6 of one mile.

KILOWATT

A unit of measure for electrical power equal to 1000 watts.

KM/H

A metric measure of speed. km/h is the abbreviation of "kilometers per hour".

45
km/h

Road sign displaying the maximum safe speed

LATITUDE

The north/south location of a position on the Earth's surface made in relation to the Earth's equator. Latitude tells us how far north or south of the equator some place is located.

We measure latitude in degrees by finding the angle between the plane of the equator and the position we are locating. The angular distance north or south from the earth's equator is measured through 90 degrees, with 90° marking the north pole and -90° marking the south pole.

Locating Positions on the Surface of the Earth

Any location on Earth is described by two numbers—its latitude and its longitude. To specify the latitude of a point on the surface:

Step 1) Picture the earth as a sphere and imagine a plane passing through the earth at the equator.
Step 2) Draw a line from the point at the center of the earth to the point you wish to locate. Find the elevation angle of that point above or below the plane of the equator. The angle of elevation is the latitude of the point.

If the point is in the *northern hemisphere* it has a positive latitude and is north of the equator; if the point is in the *southern hemisphere* it has a negative latitude and is south of the equator.

90°

Plane passing through the Equator

-90°

North Pole

Latitude 53°

53°

Plane of the Equator

Note: Longitude marks a location along a line drawn horizontally (from pole to pole) along the surface of the earth, and latitude marks a location along a vertical line drawn parallel to the equator; where the horizontal and vertical lines of a position cross, they pinpoint the exact location.

(*See* LONGITUDE)

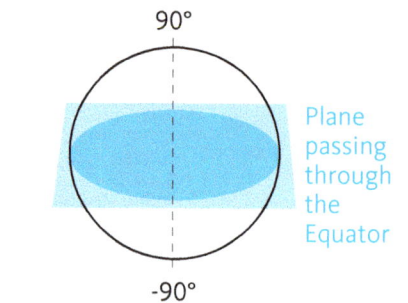

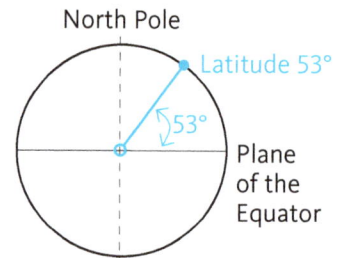

LEAST COMMON DENOMINATOR

The least common multiple of the denominators of two or more common fractions. For two or more common fractions, the smallest whole number that is a multiple of each of the denominators.

Often when calculating with fractions we must use the same denominator for each. The 'least common denominator' is the smallest number that can be used.

Example: Suppose that you would like to add together $\frac{1}{3}$, $\frac{1}{4}$ and $\frac{1}{6}$. The least common denominator of the fractions is 12.

$\frac{1}{3} = \frac{4}{12}$ $\frac{1}{4} = \frac{3}{12}$ $\frac{1}{6} = \frac{2}{12}$ $\frac{1}{3} + \frac{1}{4} + \frac{1}{6} = \frac{4}{12} + \frac{3}{12} + \frac{2}{12} = \frac{9}{12}$

LEAST COMMON MULTIPLE

The smallest natural number that is a multiple of a group of two or more numbers.

Note: The least common multiple of a group of numbers will be the smallest number that the numbers will divide leaving no remainder.

Example: The LCM of 2, 6 and 9 is 18. 18 is the smallest number that all three numbers will divide leaving no remainder.

LEGS

In a right triangle, the two sides of the triangle that are not the hypotenuse. The legs of a right triangle are the two sides that are on either side of the right (90°) angle, which is the vertex formed by the legs.

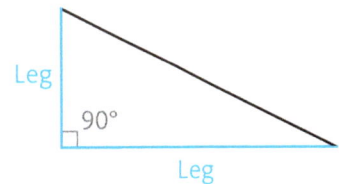

LENGTH

The measurement of something from beginning to end.

1) Length is a linear measurement, measuring the span of a geometric figure or of an object.

Examples: The length of a line segment can be measured in millimeters or inches. The length of a hallway can be measured in centimeters or yards. The length of a racetrack can be measured in kilometers or miles.

2) Length can be a measurement of a specific period of time or duration.

Example: The length of time allotted for each half in the game was twenty minutes.

(See MEASUREMENT)

LESS THAN <

The phrase and symbol used to compare two numbers when the first is smaller than the second.

Example: 3 < 5   (read three is less than five)

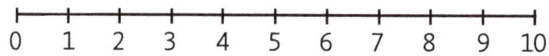

```
├──┼──┼──┼──┼──┼──┼──┼──┼──┼──┤
0   1   2   3   4   5   6   7   8   9   10
```

Example: 3 < 8 (read three is less than eight)
Note that eight is farther to the right of zero on the number line.

LESS THAN OR EQUAL TO ≤

Phrase and symbol used to compare two numbers when the first is smaller than or equal to the first.

Example: $a \leq 0$ (read **a** is less than or equal to 0)

LIKE TERMS

Terms in an algebraic expression that have all variables and the exponents of these variables alike. The numerical coefficients may vary.

Examples: In the algebraic expressions $2X^2 + 3X$ and $7X^3 + 5X^2 + 4X$
    $2X^2$ and $5X^2$ are like terms
    $3X$ and $4X$ are like terms

In the algebraic expressions $2ab^2 + 7ab - 6$ and $7ab^3 - 5ab^2 - 6ab$
    $2ab^2$ and $5ab^2$ are like terms
    $7ab$ and $6ab$ are like terms
    6 and $6ab$ have the same coefficient, but are not like terms

LINE

A straight, continuous path of points that has infinite length but no width and no depth.

Note: The CCSS state that within the standards only Euclidean geometry is addressed. In Euclidean geometry, a line is a straight set of points that extends infinitely in two directions. Two points determine a line.

Line may be defined in different ways in different geometries, but there are two important things to remember about a line:

1) It is a continuous set of points, the set of all points along its path. If you name any two points along a line, there will be an infinite number of points on the line between these points.

2) A line has only one dimension: length. In plane geometry the word 'line' is usually taken to mean a straight line. If a line is not straight, we usually refer to it as a curve or an arc.

continued ———→

LINE CONTINUED

To show the infinite length of a line, you can draw a line that goes off the edges of the page, but instead a line usually is shown with an arrow on each end; the arrows mean that the line extends in both directions to infinity.

Lines are commonly named in two ways:
1) By naming any two points on the line.

The line would be called $\overleftrightarrow{AB}$ because it passes through the two points A and B.

2) By using a single letter.

The line could also be called 'y'. By convention, this is usually a single lower case letter.

(See CURVE, GEOMETRY, PLANE GEOMETRY)

LINE OF BEST FIT

A straight line used as the best approximation of all the points in a scatter plot. The position of the line is determined by the amount of correlation between the paired variables that generate the scatter plot.

Note: In grade 6, students will sketch a line of best fit and identify if there is a positive, a negative, or no correlation between the points. Elementary students will not have to determine the equation for the line of best fit.

(See SCATTER PLOT)

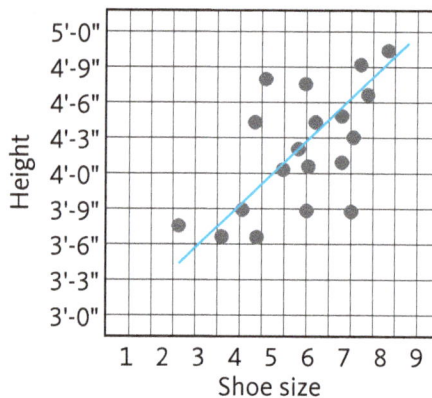

A scatter plot graphing the relationship between height and shoe size in a school room of children.

LINE OF REFLECTION

A transformation in which every point of an image appears at an equal distance on the opposite side of this line.

In a reflection the lengths of line segments and their position within the image, the measures of angles and the midpoints of the figures are unchanged.

(See TRANSFORMATION)

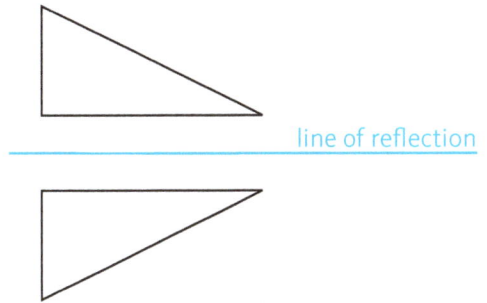

line of reflection

LINE PLOT

A graph that displays frequency using a number line.

Example: The number of siblings of each child in the third grade.

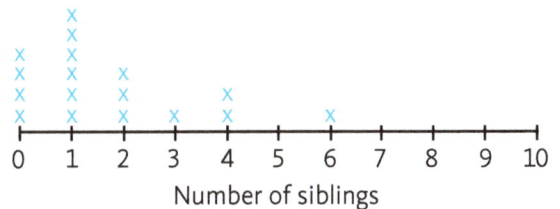

Number of siblings

LINE SYMMETRY

The property of a figure with a line that divides it into two halves that are exact mirror images of each other. If you can flip a figure over a line and the figure appears unchanged, then the figure has line symmetry. The line that you reflect or flip the image over is called the line of symmetry or the axis of symmetry.

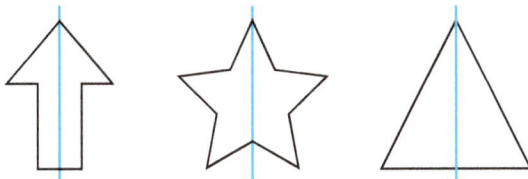

A line of symmetry divides a figure into two congruent parts

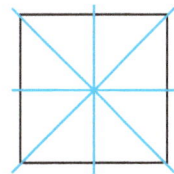

A square has 4 lines of symmetry

LINE SEGMENT

A line segment is part of a line bounded by two distinct end points and containing every point on the line between its end points.

Note: Lines extend to infinity in two directions, but line segments have two distinct endpoints.

LINEAR EQUATION

An equation that creates a straight line when it is graphed.

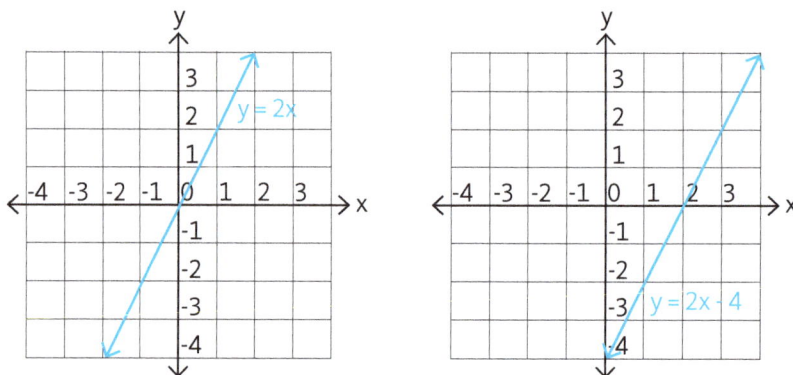

Graphs of linear equations

LITER

Unit of measurement for capacity in the metric system. Mostly used to measure liquid. Abbreviation: L

One liter is equal to one cubic decimeter and 1.0567 liquid quarts.

LOGARITHM

The power to which a fixed value, called the base of the logarithm, must be raised in order to produce a number. That is, the logarithm of any number is the exponent that shows how many times the base is multiplied by itself to produce the number.

Examples: The logarithm of 100 to base 10 is 2, because 10 to the power 2 equals 100: $100 = 10 \times 10 = 10^2$

The logarithm of 1000 to the base 10 is 3. $1000 = 10 \times 10 \times 10 = 10^3$

The logarithm of 8 to base 2 is 3 because $2 \times 2 \times 2 = 2^3 = 8$.

LONGITUDE

The distance, east to west, of the location of a position on the Earth's surface measured using vertical lines drawn along the surface of the Earth. Longitude lines run between the North and South Poles and are called meridians. They are used to calculate how far east or west of a prime meridian some place is located.

Locating Positions on the Surface of the Earth

Longitude lines are drawn north/south (or vertically) along the surface of the Earth. The Prime Meridian, which runs through Greenwich, England, is set at 0 degrees longitude. The International Date Line is halfway around the Earth's surface from this 0° line and it marks 180°.

Any location on Earth is described by two numbers—its latitude and its longitude. To specify the longitude of a point on the surface:
a) Picture the earth as a sphere. Draw the Meridians vertically along the Earth's surface from pole to pole.
b) Meridians to the west of the prime meridian are measured in the number of degrees west, and meridians to the east of the prime meridian are measured by the number of degrees east. The east/west measurement stops at the International Date Line.

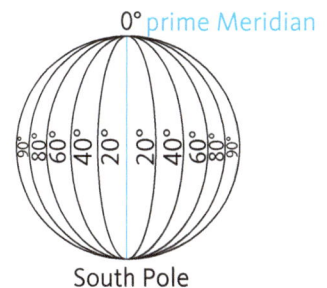

0° prime Meridian

South Pole

A point is in the *western hemisphere* if it is west of the prime meridian; the point is in the *eastern hemisphere* if it is east of the prime meridian.

continued ⟶ 139

LONGITUDE

Note: Longitude marks a location along a vertical line and latitude marks a location along a horizontal line; where the horizontal and vertical lines of a position cross, they pinpoint an exact location.

(See LATITUDE)

LOWER BOUND

The member of a set of numbers with a value equal to or less than every other member of the set.

Example: The lower bound of the set {5, 5, 7, 9, 9, 11} is 5.

LOWEST TERMS

The form of a common fraction in which the numerator and the denominator have no common factor other than 1.

Examples of fractions in lowest terms: $\frac{6}{7}$, $\frac{2}{9}$, $\frac{3}{8}$

The common fraction $\frac{3}{6}$ is not in lowest terms because it can be 'reduced' to $\frac{1}{2}$ by dividing both the numerator and the denominator by 3.

(See SIMPLEST FORM)

MAGIC SQUARE

A square of numbers in which the total of each row, each column and each diagonal equal the same number.

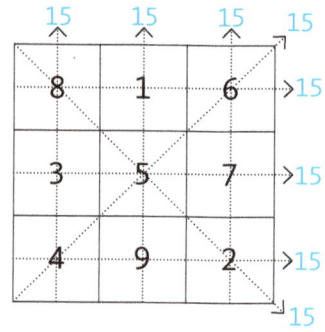

MAGNITUDE

The size or value irrespective of sign. Magnitude is the measurement of how large a mathematical term is. For the counting numbers (1, 2, 3...) the magnitude is the number itself. If a number is negative, the magnitude becomes the absolute value of the number.

Example: The magnitude of 8 is 8. The magnitude of -8 becomes the absolute value of -8, which is 8. In both cases, the magnitude is the distance from zero on a number line. Both 8 and -8 are a distance of 8 away from zero.

MAJOR ARC

When two points on a circle define arcs of different lengths, the longer arc is called the major arc.

(See ARC, MINOR ARC)

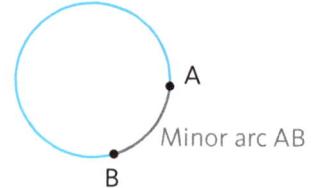

Major arc AB

A

Minor arc AB

B

MAJOR AXIS

The longest diameter of an ellipse.

The major axis will pass through the center of the ellipse and through both foci.

(See ELLIPSE)

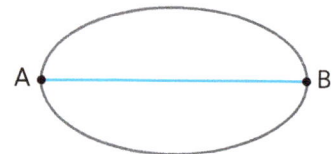

Line segment $\overline{AB}$ is the major axis of this ellipse

MAPPING

A rule which relates each element of one set to a unique element in another set.

In mathematics, the first set is referred to as the domain and the second set is the range. Pairing each member of the domain with one and only one member of the range is the process of mapping. If each element in the domain is paired with one and only one element in the range, the rule that defines the relation between the two sets is a function.

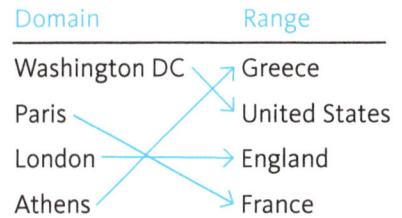

Domain	Range
Washington DC	Greece
Paris	United States
London	England
Athens	France

(See FUNCTION)

MASS

A measure of the amount of matter in an object. Because the most frequent process of finding mass requires weighing, we often confuse mass with weight. But weight is actually a measurement of the force of gravity on an object and not a quantity of mass. Weight can change depending on where you are (such as if you were on the moon) while mass remains the same.

(See WEIGHT)

MEAN

The most commonly used average of a set of numbers.

(See ARITHMETIC MEAN, AVERAGE)

MEASURE OF CENTRAL TENDENCY

A measure that attempts to find the middle of a group of data. The three most common measures of central tendency are the mean, the median, and the mode.

(See ARITHMETIC MEAN, MEDIAN, MODE)

MEASURE OF VARIATION

A measure that describes the scatter or variation of a set of data. It is also known as measure of spread. There are three measures of variation: range; variance; and standard deviation.

MEASUREMENT

A comparison between an attribute (such as length or weight) and a unit of measure for that attribute.

Measurements are made by comparing an attribute to a standard measurement for that attribute. Example: a meter or yard when measuring length or a kilogram or pound when measuring weight. Attributes of dimension, quantity, or capacity are all determined by comparing them with the standard.

In the common or customary measurement system:
    length is measured in inches, feet, yards, and miles;
    capacity is measured in cups, pints, quarts, and gallons;
    weight is measured in ounces, pounds, and tons;
    temperature is measured in degrees Fahrenheit.

In the decimal based metric system, all standard measures are increased in powers of ten.

Example: 1 kilometer = 10 decimeters = 100 meters

Angles are measured in degrees. There are 360° around a circle.

Examples of different measures:

A •————————————• B

Line segment $\overline{AB}$ measures
1.5 inches in length

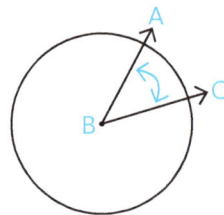

Angle ABC measures 45°

MEDIAN

1) In a set of data, the central value such that there are just as many numbers greater than it as are less than it. To find the median, first place the numbers in order of value. If the set has an odd number of items then the median is in middle number. If the set has an even number of items, then the median is the mean of the two middle numbers.

Example: In the set of numbers {2, 6, 7, 10, 11}, 7 is the median.

2) The line segment from a vertex of a triangle to the midpoint of the opposite side.

Example: Line segment AM is the median of the triangle.

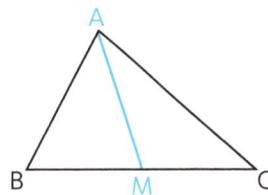

MEMBER

Any element contained in a set is a member of that set. The symbol ∈ is used to denote the member of a set.

Example: B∈{A, B, C, D}

(See SET)

MERIDIAN

Semicircles drawn on the surface of the Earth that connect the north pole and the south pole and cross the equator at a right angle. The prime meridian, which is considered 0°, is the meridian that passes through Greenwich, England.

(To understand the way we locate positions on the Earth's surface, see LATITIUDE and LONGITUDE.)

METER

A unit of measurement of length in the metric system of measures. Abbreviation: m

1 meter = 100 centimeters
1 meter = 39.37 inches

(See LENGTH, METRIC SYSTEM OF MEASUREMENT)

METRIC SYSTEM OF MEASUREMENT

A decimal based system of weights and measures. The metric system is used universally in science, and is the official system of measurement in many countries.

(See MEASUREMENT)

METRIC TON

A unit of weight in the metric system of measurement.

1 metric ton is equal to about 2,200 pounds.
1 metric ton = 1000 kilograms

MIDNIGHT

12:00 a.m. Midnight signifies the end of one day and the beginning of the next.

MIDPOINT

The midpoint of a line segment is the point in the middle of the line, exactly halfway between the two endpoints.

(See ENDPOINT)

MILE

A unit of length in the common or customary system of measurement.
Abbreviation: mi

1 mile is equal to about 1.609 kilometers.
1 mile = 5280 feet

MILLENNIUM

A period of time of a thousand years.

Example: All the years from 2000 to 2999 are a millennium.

MILLI-

A prefix meaning one thousandth or $\frac{1}{1000}$.

1 millimeter = .001 meter
1 milliliter = .001 liter

MILLIGRAM

A unit of measurement of weight in the metric system of measures.

1 milligram is equal to $\frac{1}{1000}$ gram.
1 milligram = .001 gram

(See WEIGHT, METRIC SYSTEM OF MEASUREMENT)

MILLILITER

A unit of measurement of capacity in the metric system of measures.

1 milliliter is equal to $\frac{1}{1000}$ liter.
1 milliliter = .001 liter

(See CAPACITY, METRIC SYSTEM OF MEASUREMENT)

MILLIMETER

A unit of measurement of length in the metric system of measures.

1 millimeter is equal to $\frac{1}{1000}$ meter.
1 millimeter = .001 meter

(See LENGTH, METRIC SYSTEM OF MEASUREMENT)

MILLION

A million is a thousand thousands (1,000,000).

MINIMUM

The smallest or the least value in a given set of data.

MINOR ARC

The shorter arc joining two points on the circumference (edge) of a circle.

(See ARC, MAJOR ARC)

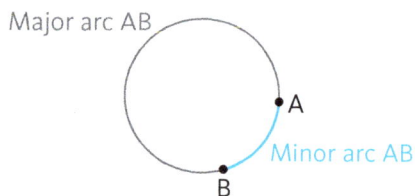

Major arc AB

A

Minor arc AB

B

MINOR AXIS

The shortest diameter of an ellipse. The minor axis extends from one side of the ellipse to the other, passing through the center.

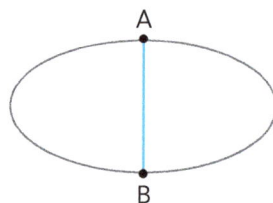

A

B

Line segment $\overline{AB}$ is the minor axis of this ellipse

MINUEND

In the arithmetic operation of subtraction, the number that is subtracted from.

The components in a subtraction problem are called the minuend, the subtrahend and the difference: minuend − subtrahend = difference.

Example: 15 − 7 = 8   In this problem 15 is the minuend.

(See SUBTRAHEND)

MINUS

To subtract or take away. The minus sign (-) is used to represent subtraction.

Example: Nine minus seven is written 9 − 7 symbolically. 9 − 7 = 2.

(See MINUS SIGN)

MINUS SIGN (-)

1) Indicates the arithmetic operation of subtraction.

Example: 15 − 7 = 8

2) Shows that a number is in the negative direction on the number line. Negative numbers are those below zero.

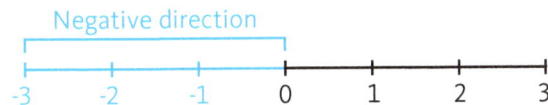

Negative direction

-3   -2   -1   0   1   2   3

MINUTE

1) A unit of measurement for time. A minute is a short period of time.

60 seconds = 1 minute
60 minutes = 1 hour

2) A unit of measurement for angles. To measure angles in increments smaller than degrees, each degree is divided into 60 minutes.

60 minutes = 1 degree

MIXED NUMBER

(sometimes called MIXED DECIMAL or MIXED FRACTION)
A number with both a whole and fractional parts. The fractional part may be a common fraction or a fraction in decimal form.

Examples of mixed numbers: $1\frac{1}{2}$ $24\frac{1}{4}$ 12.78   4.051

(See COMMON FRACTION, DECIMAL FRACTION)

MOBIUS STRIP

A surface with only one side.

To make a Mobius strip, cut a long strip of paper from any sheet and put the two narrow ends of the strip together forming a loop. Now turn one side half way, so that the strip has one twist in it and the front side of the paper is joined to the back. Tape the two ends together, keeping the twist. The strip now has just one side. Take a pencil and draw a continuous line along the strip. You will be able to return to your starting point without turning the paper.

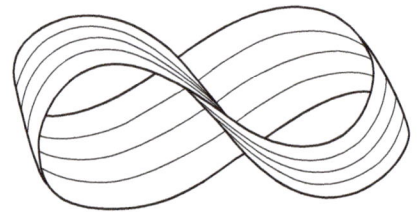

MODE
In a set of numbers, the number that appears most frequently.

Example: {89, 95, 73, 69, 89, 82, 91, 89, 87, 83}   In this set of test scores, 89 is the mode.

Note: A set of data can have more than one mode and not every data set will have a mode.

MONEY
A medium that can be exchanged in return for goods and/or services. Money is usually used as a measure of the value of goods or services.

Note: The official currency, coins and paper bills, issued by a government is the money of that government.

MONOMIAL
An algebraic expression containing only one term.

Examples: $5y^2$ ab^3

$9x + 3$ is a binomial that contains two terms, $9x$ and 3. In this example $9x$ and 3 are monomials.

MONTH
A unit of measurement for time. 1 year is divided into 12 months, but months vary in length from 28 to 31 days.

MULTIPLE
The product of two whole numbers.

Examples: The multiples of 3 are 3, 6, 9, 12....
          The multiples of 5 are 5, 10, 15, 20....

MULTIPLICATION

The operation of repeated addition. In performing the operation of multiplication, a x b, a is added to itself b times.

Note: Multiplication tells you how many times you have a given number.

Example: 4 x 3 = 12 This multiplication operation actually means that 3 is added to itself 4 times (3 + 3 + 3 + 3 = 12) or that we have four threes.

Because the factors in a multiplication operation can be in any order (multiplication is a commutative operation) it can also be thought of as adding 4 to itself 3 times (4 + 4 + 4 = 12) or that we have three fours.

When we multiply by a fraction, we essentially say that we have only part of a number.

Examples: $\frac{1}{2}$ x 3 = $1\frac{1}{2}$
This multiplication tells us how many times we have 3, or put another way, how many threes we have. We only have $\frac{1}{2}$ of 3.

$4\frac{1}{2}$ x 3 = 13.5
In this multiplication, 3 is added to itself $4\frac{1}{2}$ times (3 + 3 + 3 + 3 + $1\frac{1}{2}$ = 13.5)

MULTIPLICATION TABLE

A table that displays the results of multiplying any two numbers listed across the top and down the side of the table. Commonly, numbers to be multiplied are written along the top row and down the first column, and the results of the multiplication of the numbers are written where their row and column meet.

x	1	2	3	4	5	6	7	8	9	10
1	1	2	3	4	5	6	7	8	9	10
2	2	4	6	8	10	12	14	16	18	20
3	3	6	9	12	15	18	21	24	27	30
4	4	8	12	16	20	24	28	32	36	40
5	5	10	15	20	25	30	35	40	45	50
6	6	12	18	24	30	36	42	48	54	60
7	7	14	21	28	35	42	49	56	63	70
8	8	16	24	32	40	48	56	64	72	80
9	9	18	27	36	45	54	63	72	81	90
10	10	20	30	40	50	60	70	80	90	100

MULTIPLICATIVE IDENTITY

1 is the multiplicative identity because multiplying any number by 1 leaves the number unchanged: for any number a, a × 1 = a.

Examples: $5 \times 1 = 5$ $17 \times 1 = 17$

MULTIPLICATIVE INVERSE

Another name for a reciprocal. When you multiply a number by its multiplicative inverse the result is 1.

Examples: $5 \times \frac{1}{5} = 1$ $a \times \frac{1}{a} = 1$

MULTIPLY

An arithmetic operation of repeated additions. When you multiply, you add the same number to itself several times.

(See MULTIPLICATION)

MUTUALLY EXCLUSIVE

Two events that cannot occur at the same time.

Example: It is impossible to toss one coin and have the result be both a head and a tail at the same time. The results are mutually exclusive.

N

n
A letter often used to stand for an unknown number.

Example: n + 4 = 9   (n = 5)

NATURAL NUMBER
The set of whole numbers beginning with 1: 1, 2, 3, 4...∞

The natural numbers can be thought of as the number 1 and all other numbers obtained by adding 1 repeatedly, so negative numbers and fractions are not part of the set. These are sometimes called the counting numbers.

NEGATIVE
Having a value less than 0. Negative numbers are written with a minus sign (-) in front.

Example: The temperature today is -2° Celsius.

NEGATIVE INTEGER
An integer with a value less than 0.

(See INTEGER, NEGATIVE NUMBER)

NEGATIVE NUMBER
Any number that is less than 0. Negative numbers are below 0 on the number line.

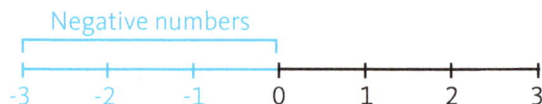

Negative numbers

-3   -2   -1   0   1   2   3

NET

1) A pattern that can be cut and folded into a model of a solid shape.

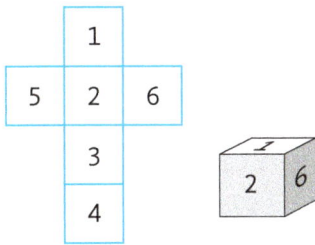

Net of a cube

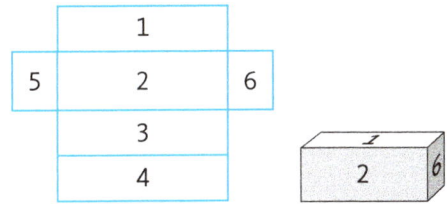

Net of a rectangular prism

2) Everything that remains after all deductions have been made.

Examples:

Net Profits: The profits remaining after all deductions have been made for expenses.

Net Weight: The weight of the contents of a package after the weight of all of the packaging has been deducted.

Net Worth: How much a company or a person owns (their assets) minus how much they owe to others (liabilities).

NICKEL

A coin with the value $\frac{1}{20}$ of a U.S. dollar. A nickel is worth five cents and is written 5¢ or $0.05

NONAGON

A polygon with nine sides.

(See POLYGON)

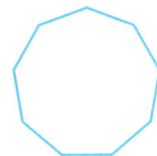

NONAHEDRON
A polyhedron with nine faces.

Elongated
square pyramid

Elongated
triangular pyramid

Octagonal
pyramid

NONLINEAR EQUATION
An equation whose graph does not form a straight line.

(See LINEAR EQUATION)

NONREPEATING DECIMAL
A decimal that does not repeat in any pattern nor terminate. We call these numbers irrational because they cannot be accurately written as a ratio of one number to another.

Example: The number π has a value of 3.14159.... The decimal does not repeat in a pattern nor terminate. π is the ratio of the circumference of a circle to its diameter and it is an irrational number.

(See IRRATIONAL NUMBER, NONTERMINATING DECIMAL)

NONTERMINATING DECIMAL
A decimal that has no end. Nonterminating decimals can repeat in a pattern or be nonrepeating.

Examples: Repeating $\frac{1}{3}$ is equal to .3333333...∞

Nonrepeating   The number π has a value of 3.14159....

(See IRRATIONAL NUMBER, NONREPEATING DECIMAL)

NORMAL DISTRIBUTION

The distribution of a set of data that has little tendency to produce unusually extreme values. For example, the height of all adult human beings falls within a certain range with very few exceptions falling outside that normal range.

A bell curve is used to graph the mathematical concept called normal distribution. The center of the curve contains the greatest concentration of the data and is the highest point on the arc of the graph. The normal data is concentrated in the center of the graph and decreases on either side.

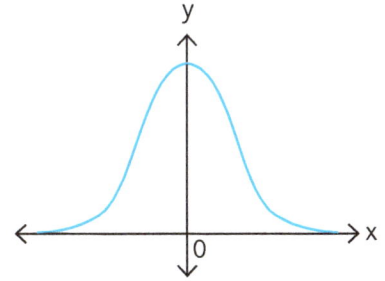

Normal distribution graph, called a bell shaped curve

NOT EQUAL ≠

Indicates that two numbers do not have the same value.

Examples: $5 \neq 7$; $\frac{1}{2} \neq \frac{3}{8}$

nth

1) The general name for a term in a sequence.

Example: In the sequence 1, 3, 6, 9, ... each term increases by a 3. A general name for any term (n) except the first term could be written as n = (n - 1) x 3. If we substitute 4 for n, the 4th term would be: (4 - 1) x 3 or 9. If we substitute 5 for n the 5th term would be: (5 - 1) x 3 or 12. This general formula allows us to find any term.

2) A general term used to indicate that a number will be multiplied by itself an indefinite number (n) of times.

Example: 7^n is read as 7 to the nth power. X^n is read as X to the nth power.

(See POWER, SEQUENCE)

NUMBER

A mathematical concept (or idea) used to quantify or order. We use the concept of number to count, measure, arrange and label. A notational symbol representing a number is called a numeral.

In common usage, the word *number* can mean the abstract concept, the symbol or the word we use for a certain number.

(See NUMERAL, NUMERATION SYSTEM)

NUMBER LINE

A line with points that graph all real numbers in order, including negative numbers and fractions. The distance between any two consecutive integers on a number line graph must be consistent.

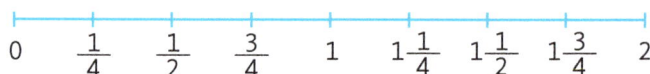

NUMBER PATTERN

A list of numbers that follow a certain rule.

Examples of different types of number patterns:
Arithmetic Sequence: A pattern formed by constantly adding the same number to (or subtracting the same number from) the first number in the sequence.

      1, 3, 5, 7, 9...   (adding 2)
      44, 33, 22....   (subtracting 11)

In an arithmetic sequence the members would all be the same distance apart on a number line.

Geometric Sequence: A pattern formed by constantly multiplying each new member by the same number.

      1, 2, 4, 8, 16.... (multiplying by 2)
      1, 3, 9, 27....   (multiplying by 3)

(See ORDER, PATTERN, SERIES, SEQUENCE)

NUMBER SENTENCE

An expression that includes numbers and operation symbols and must include a relational symbol such as = (equal to); > (greater than); <, (less than); etc.

Note: Number sentences can be true (3 < 12) or false (3 + 6 = 22).

Examples: $3 + 4 = 7$; $27 > 24$; $a^2 + a^3 = b \div 7$; $A \geq 27$

NUMBER SYSTEM

A number system is a way of identifying the quantity of something and of defining order. A number system includes a set of symbols used to express quantities as the basis for counting, determining order, comparing amounts, performing calculations and representing value and a set of mathematical rules that are used to calculate. Both the symbols and the rules are parts of the number system.

(See DECIMAL NUMBER SYSTEM)

NUMERAL

A symbol used to represent a number. Throughout history, different numerals have been used to represent the same number.

Examples: In the Roman system, V represents the number we write as 5.

Using tally marks, the number 5 can be represented as ЖИ

In ancient Egypt, a man with raised hands (the astonished man) was the numeral used for 1,000,000.

NUMERATION SYSTEM

A set of symbols used to express numbers. A system of numeration is used to name numbers, write numbers, count and calculate. Systems for numeration include the rules used within the system to perform operations such as adding and subtracting.

Examples: The Egyptians created a numeration system based on groups of ten. It was used over 5000 years ago. These are some of the symbols they used to represent numbers.

One Staff	Ten Heelbone	Hundred Scroll	Thousand Lotus Flower

(See NUMBER SYSTEM)

NUMERATOR

1) One of the terms in a fraction, the numerator is the number that is written above the fraction bar. The word numerator is taken from the word number; the numerator of a fraction tells us (names) the number of parts we have.

Note that the denominator tells us the total number of parts the whole has been divided into; the numerator tells us how many parts of that whole we have.

Example: In the fraction $\frac{3}{5}$, the denominator (or the 5) indicates that the whole is divided into 5 equal parts. The numerator tells us that we have 3 of these parts.

2) The first number of a ratio.

(See DENOMINATOR, FRACTION, RATIO)

NUMERICAL EXPRESSION

A mathematical phrase involving only numbers and one or more operational symbols. A numerical expression does not include a relational symbol.

Example: 8 + 3 is a numerical expression. 8 + 3 = 11 is a number sentence.

(See NUMBER SENTENCE)

OBELUS (÷)

The symbol primarily used to indicate the operation division. It is the sign used as the division operator in elementary arithmetic.

OBLIQUE

1) Slanted. Not truly horizontal or vertical.

Example: Shapes distorted by sliding the top to one side so that the top is not directly above the bottom are oblique.

Oblique cylinder

2) Lines or planes that are neither parallel nor perpendicular.

Example: Lines in a plane that are oblique.

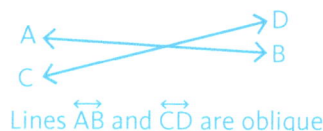

Lines $\overleftrightarrow{AB}$ and $\overleftrightarrow{CD}$ are oblique

(See ACUTE, PARALLEL, PERPENDICULAR)

OBLIQUE ANGLE

Any angle that is not a right angle.

OBLIQUE TRIANGLE

A triangle that does not contain a right angle.

OBTUSE ANGLE

An angle between 90° and 180°. Obtuse angles are less pointed than acute angles.

(See ACUTE)

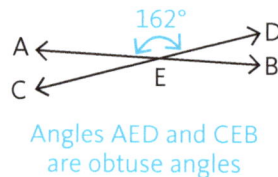

Angles AED and CEB are obtuse angles

OBTUSE TRIANGLE

A triangle in which one of the angles is obtuse (more than 90° and less than 180°).

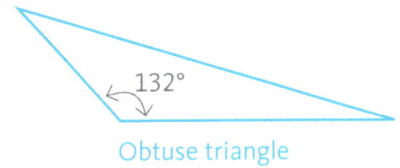

132°

Obtuse triangle

OCTAGON

A polygon that has 8 sides.

Example: A regular octagon is a polygon that has eight equal sides and eight equal angles.

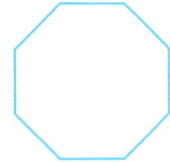

Regular octagon

OCTAHEDRON

A polyhedron that has eight polygonal faces. A regular octahedron is one of the Platonic Solids.

Example: A regular octahedron is a polyhedron that has eight equilateral triangles as its faces.

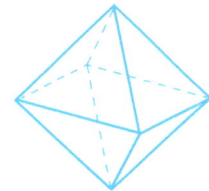

Regular octahedron

(See PLATONIC SOLIDS)

OCTAL

A number system based on the number 8. There are 8 digits in an octal number system with values of 0 through 7. When using this place value system, the number 8 is represented by 10 and each place represents powers of 8.

(See DECIMAL NUMBER SYSTEM, PLACE VALUE)

ODD NUMBER

Any integer that when divided by 2 leaves a remainder of 1. Odd numbers will end in 1, 3, 5, 7, or 9.

Example: Three Blind Mice. Odd numbers are numbers that don't divide into pairs.

(See EVEN NUMBER)

ODDS

An expression of the likelihood of an event occurring. Odds is a ratio that compares the number of favorable outcomes of an event to the number of unfavorable outcomes.

The odds in favor of an event can be determined by dividing the possible number of favorable outcomes by the number of all possible outcomes minus the possible number of favorable outcomes.

$$\text{odds} = \frac{\text{probability of event}}{(\text{all possible outcomes } - \text{ probability of event})}$$

Example: There are 6 sides on a die. The odds of rolling a 2 on a fair six-sided die are 1 to 5 (1 divided by 6 − 1), which can be expressed as 1:5 or as $\frac{1}{5}$.

ODOMETER

An instrument that measures and records distance traveled. Odometers are found on the instrument panels of cars.

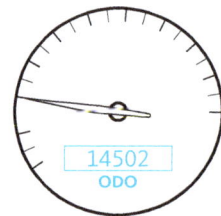

14502
ODO

ONE DIMENSIONAL

In geometry, a figure having only one dimension: length. Lines, rays and line segments have only length and no width, and are one dimensional.

(See DIMENSION)

ONE TO ONE CORRESPONDENCE

Every element of one set is paired with one and only one element from the other set.

(See ELEMENT, SET)

OPEN CURVE

A curve whose ends do not meet.

Example: A parabola is an open curve.

OPEN SENTENCE

A mathematical sentence that contains at least one missing value. In an open sentence, more information is needed to make the sentence true or false.

Example: $6 + X = 17$ is an open sentence. Only including the proper value of X will make the sentence true.

OPEN SET

A set in which the limits that define the set are not members of the set.

Example: The set of real numbers between 3 and 9 is an open set because the numbers 3 and 9 are not members of the set.

OPERATION

A process of carrying out rules of procedure to determine a result. As mathematical processes applied to solve a specific problem, the basic operations of arithmetic are addition, subtraction, multiplication, and division.

OPPOSITE ANGLES

When two lines intersect, four angles are formed. The two angles directly opposite to each other are called opposite angles. Opposite angles are always non-adjacent.

(See ADJACENT)

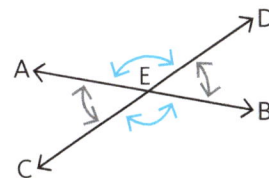

AEC and BED are opposite angles.
CEB and AED are opposite angles.

OPPOSITE NUMBERS

Numbers that are the same distance from zero on the number line, but in opposite directions.

When opposite numbers are added, the sum is zero.

Example: 6 and -6 are opposite numbers.

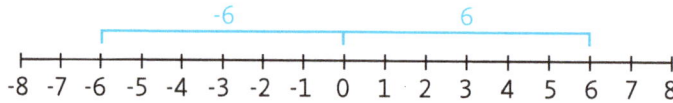

OPPOSITE SIDE

In a triangle, the side facing a given angle. It is the only side of the triangle that does not form the vertex of the angle.

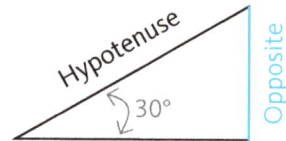

Example: Side opposite the 30° angle.

In a quadrilateral, opposite sides are sides that do not share a common vertex.

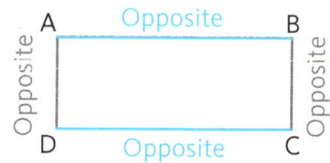

ORDER

To arrange a given set by numerical value, physical size or other quality that can be quantitated.

Example: The coach had the team line up in order of their height.

ORDER OF ROTATIONAL SYMMETRY

The number of different positions a figure can be rotated into, without making any changes to the way it looks originally.

An equilateral triangle can be rotated into 3 different positions, each of which looks exactly the same. It has an order of rotational symmetry of 3. A square has an order of rotational symmetry of 4, but a non-square rectangle has an order of rotational symmetry of only 2.

(See SYMMETRY)

3

Equilateral triangle

4

Square

2

Non-square rectangle

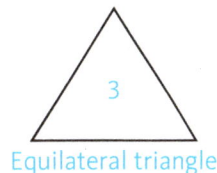

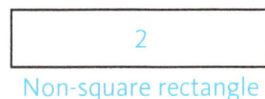

Orders of rotational symmetry

ORDER OF OPERATIONS

When working on a mathematical expression, the order in which we perform arithmetical operations. If the correct order of operations is not followed, it can lead to different solutions of the same expression.

The rules for performing operations in the correct order are:
1. Evaluate all expressions written inside parentheses.
2. Evaluate all exponential expressions.
3. Perform all multiplications and/or divisions from left to right.
4. Perform all additions and/or subtractions from left to right.

Most people suggest using the following sentence to help you remember the correct order: **P**lease **E**xcuse **M**y **D**ear **A**unt **S**ally. **P**arenthesis, **E**xponents, **M**ultiplication, **D**ivision, **A**ddition, **S**ubtraction.

Example: $7 + (13 - 5) \times 10 \div 2 \ = \ 7 + \mathbf{(8)} \times 10 \div 2 \ = \ 7 + \mathbf{80} \div 2 \ = \ 7 + \mathbf{40} \ = \ 47$

ORDERED PAIRS

A system used to locate the positions of points on a two-dimensional surface. Ordered pairs are used to name locations on maps and in geometric coordinate systems.

Example: An XY coordinate system, sometimes called a Cartesian frame, consists of two perpendicular axes that cross at a central point called the origin. Positions on the plane are determined according to their distance from the origin and each location is given by an ordered pair.

Using this coordinate system we would locate the point to the right by the ordered pair (3, -1), meaning that it is located at a distance of 3 from 0 along the x axis and -1 from 0 along the y axis. You can see that the order of the pair is important because the point (-1, 3) names a different location.

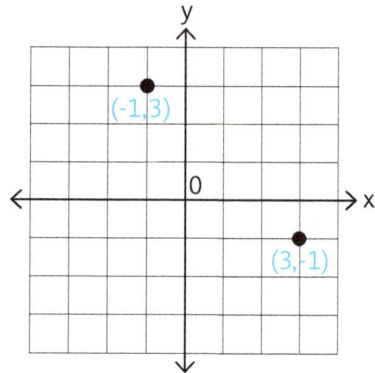

In a three-dimensional space, 3 coordinates, (x, y, z) give the location of a point. This is called an ordered triple.

(See AXIS, CARTESIAN COORDINATE SYSTEM, ORIGIN)

ORDINAL NUMBERS

Numbers that name the position of something in a list.

The ordinal numbers: 1st, 2nd, 3rd, 4th, 5th...∞

ORDINATE

The name for the vertical (y) value in a pair of coordinates. The ordinate locates how far up or down the y axis a point lies and is always written second in an ordered pair.

Example: In the ordered pair (3, -1) the ordinate is -1 and locates the point at 1 line below the x axis.

(See ORDERED PAIRS)

ORIGIN

A starting point.

Number line origin

On a number line the origin is at 0.

In a two dimensional coordinate system, the origin is the point of intersection of the x and y axis. The coordinates of the origin are (0, 0). The location of any point is found by counting the distance along the two coordinates beginning at the origin.

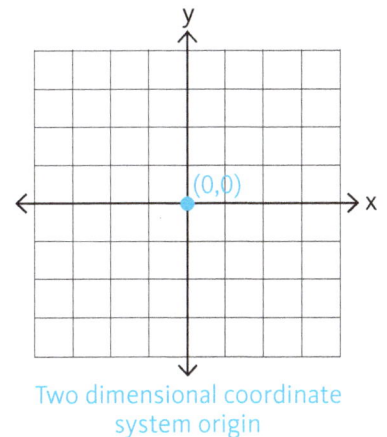

Two dimensional coordinate system origin

In a three dimensional coordinate system the origin is the point (0, 0, 0).

(See AXIS, CARTESIAN COORDINATE SYSTEM, COORDINATES, NUMBER LINE)

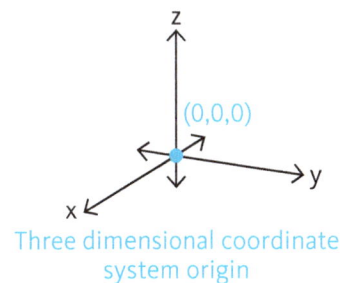

Three dimensional coordinate system origin

ORTHOCENTER

The point of intersection of the altitudes of a triangle.

(See ALTITUDE)

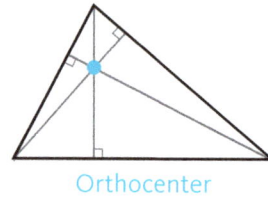

Orthocenter

OUNCE

A unit of measure of mass in the customary measurement system. An ounce is equivalent to about half the weight of a normal size hen's egg.

Note: This is not the same unit of measure as a fluid ounce, which is a measure of capacity (volume).

(See MASS, MEASUREMENT, WEIGHT))

OUTCOME

A possible result of a probability experiment.

Examples: If a die is thrown, there are six possible outcomes. One possible outcome is 4, another is 6.

If a coin is tossed, there are only two possible outcomes, heads or tails.

OUTLIER

An element of a data set that, because of its value, stands out from the rest of the data.

Example: In the data set (1, 3, 5, 2, 6, 22, 9, 3, 3), the value 22 is an outlier. If used to find an average, it would skew the average of the data.

OVAL

Another term for an ellipse. Oval is not, properly, a term used in mathematics.

(See ELLIPSE)

PAIR

Two entities similar in form and/or function which are used together as a single entity.

(See ORDERED PAIR)

PALINDROME

Words or numbers that read the same from left to right and from right to left. From the Greek *palindromes*, running back again, in mathematics palindromic numbers read the same in both directions.

Examples: 1001, 2332, 464 and 12221 are palindromic numbers.

PARABOLA

A parabola is a curve in which every point on the curve is at an equal distance from:
a) a fixed point called the *focus* **and**
b) a fixed straight line called the *directrix*.

The axis of symmetry of a parabola goes through the focus, at right angles to the directrix.

Note: If you fire a missile or throw a stone into the air it will arc upward and then arc down again following the path of a parabola.

(See AXIS OF SYMMETRY, CONIC SECTION, FOCUS)

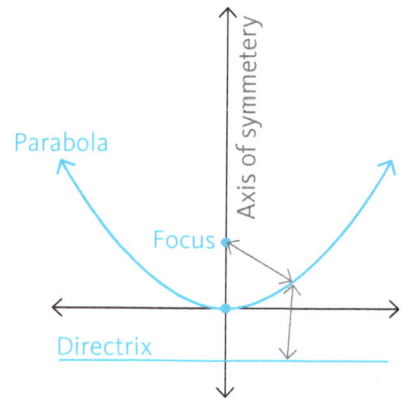

Every point on the parabola is the same distance from the focus and from the directrix

PARABOLOID

A surface formed by rotating a parabola around its axis of symmetry.

(See AXIS OF SYMMETRY, PARABOLA)

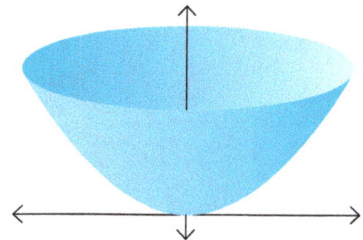

PARALLEL LINES

Different lines that lie in the same plane and never intersect or cross each other. The symbol we use to indicate that lines are parallel is **ll**.

(See INTERSECT)

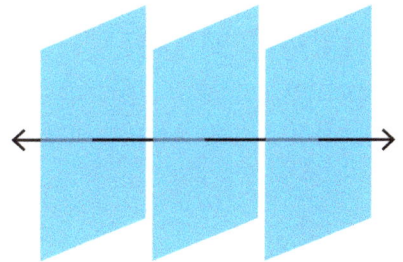

A •————————————• B
C •————————————• D
E •————————————• F

PARALLEL PLANES

Planes in space that never intersect each other.

(See INTERSECT)

PARALLELEPIPED

A polyhedron with six faces each of which is a parallelogram and with opposite faces lying in parallel planes.

(See PARALLELOGRAM, POLYHEDRON)

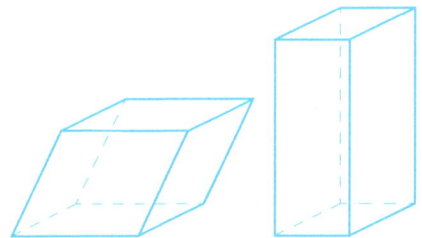

PARALLELOGRAM

A four sided polygon in which the two pairs of opposite sides are parallel. The opposite sides of a parallelogram are equal.

(See POLYGON, QUADRILATERAL)

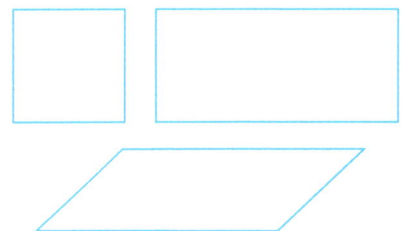

PARENTHESES

Brackets used to change the normal order of operations by grouping together terms with operations which must be completed before other operations. The singular of parentheses is parenthesis.

Example: $3 \times 8 + 6 = \textbf{24} + 6 = 30$ but $3 \times (8 + 6) = 3 \times \textbf{14} = 42$

PARTIAL PRODUCT ALGORITHM

The process of multiplying the multiplicand by parts of the multiplier when the multiplier is more than one digit, and then adding together these partial products.

Example: Decomposing factors into the sum of smaller products often simplifies multi-digit multiplication.

23×37 can be decomposed into $(20 + 3) \times (30 + 7)$

Multiplying by the unit position of the multiplier we have:
$7 \times (20 + 3) = (7 \times 20) + (7 \times 3) = 140 + 21 = 161$
Multiplying by the tens position of the multiplier we have:
$30 \times (20 + 3) = (30 \times 20) + (30 \times 3) = 600 + 90 = 690$

$161 + 690 = 851$

(See DECOMPOSE)

PARTITIVE DIVISION

Partitive division separates a quantity into a specified number of equal parts. Partitive division is sometimes called equal groups or sharing.

Example: There are 24 candies. Each of 3 friends receives the same number of candies. How many candies does each friend receive?

$24 \div 3 = 8$

An array of 24 candies partitioned into 3 rows of 8 each.

(See DIVISION)

PASCAL'S TRIANGLE

A triangular array of numbers in which each number is the sum of the two numbers directly above it, one above to the left and the other above to the right.

Named for Blaise Pascal (1623-1662) a French mathematician, physicist and religious philosopher, each row in a Pascal's triangle starts and ends with 1. Pascal's triangle can be extended to infinity.

PATTERN

A repeating or growing sequence or design arranged by following a given rule.

Patterns in mathematics include: an arithmetic sequence, a number pattern in which there is a constant difference between consecutive members in the pattern; and a geometric pattern which multiplies each consecutive member by a constant.

Another example of pattern is the Fibonacci sequence in which each number equals the sum of the two numbers before it.

Many patterns are also created by geometric shapes.

The leaves of many plants are arranged in a pattern

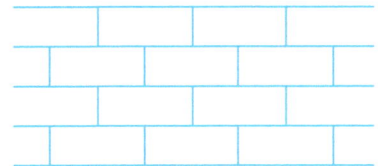

Patterns are often found in brickwork (above), fences, and windows

(See ARITHMETIC SEQUENCE, ARRAY, ATTRIBUTE PATTERN, FIBONACCI SEQUENCE, GEOMETRIC SEQUENCE, SEQUENCE, TESSELLATION)

PECK

A unit of dry measure in the United States, a peck is equal to 8 dry quarts, or 537.6 cubic inches (8.810 liters).

4 pecks = 1 bushel

(See DRY MEASURE)

PENNY

A coin with the value $\frac{1}{100}$ of a U.S. dollar. A penny is worth one cent and written 1¢ or $0.01.

PENTAGON

A polygon with five sides.

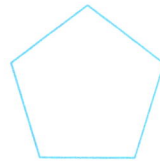

Regular pentagon because all the sides and angles are the same

Irregular concave pentagon

PENTAGONAL NUMBER

A whole number that can be represented in an array that has the shape of a pentagon.

(See FIGURATE NUMBERS)

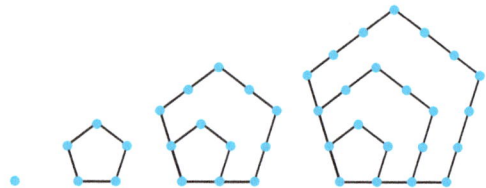

Pentagonal numbers 1, 5, 12, 22

PENTAGRAM

A figure in a plane constructed by connecting the vertices of a pentagon with straight lines.

PERCENT %

A ratio that represents parts of 100. A percent is a fraction with a denominator of 100 that compares a quantity to 100, which is the whole. That is, 100% is equal to the entire amount or the whole, so 10% is actually $\frac{10}{100}$ or one tenth of the whole. 25% is the equivalent of $\frac{25}{100}$ or $\frac{1}{4}$ of the whole.

Examples: If the state sales tax is 5%, the state collects an additional $0.05 every time you spend a dollar.

The air we breathe is 21% oxygen. 79% of our air is composed of other gasses.

(See DECIMAL)

PERCENTILE

A value on a scale that indicates the percent of the distribution that is equal to or below it.

For example, a score at the 95th percentile is equal to or better than 95 percent of the other scores in the group being evaluated.

PERFECT NUMBER

A number that is equal to the sum of the proper divisors of the number itself.

Example: The proper divisors of 6 are 1, 2, and 3. 1 + 2 + 3 = 6
6 is a perfect number. 28 is also a perfect number.

PERFECT SQUARE

A number made by squaring another whole number.

9 is a perfect square because $3^2 = 9$. 16 is a perfect square because $4^2 = 16$.

PERIMETER

The distance around a two-dimensional shape. The perimeter measures the distance round the outer edges of a shape in a plane.

Note: The perimeter of a circle is called its circumference.

(See CIRCUMFERENCE)

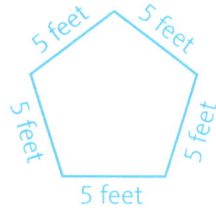

Since each side of this regular pentagon measures 5 feet, the perimeter of the pentagon is 25 feet

---

PERMUTATION

Possible arrangements of a set of objects in which the order of the arrangement makes a difference; an arrangement of a set of objects into a particular order.

Note: In mathematics we use precise language when we group a set of objects. If the order of the members of the set doesn't matter, it is called a combination. If the order of the members does matter it is a called a permutation.

The number of different ways of arranging objects from a set of different objects when the order is important is computed using a factorial. A factorial is the result of multiplying together the number of objects from 1 up to and including that number.

Example: How many ways can you arrange the letters A, B and C?
Because there are 3 members of the set {A, B, C} there are
$3 \times 2 \times 1$ or 6 different orders in which they can be arranged:
ABC, ACB, BAC, BCA, CAB, CBA

A set with 4 distinct members could be arranged in
$4 \times 3 \times 2 \times 1$ or 24 different orders.

(See COMBINATION, FACTORIAL)

PERPENDICULAR

Meeting at right angles (90° angles).

(See PERPENDICULAR LINES, PERPENDICULAR PLANES)

PERPENDICULAR LINES

Lines that cross at right angles (90° angles); line segments that meet at right angles.

In drawings, 90° angles are indicated by a small square at the corner of the two sides.

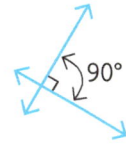

Perpendicular lines

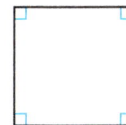

Corners of a square are formed by perpendicular line segments

PERPENDICULAR PLANES

Planes that intersect at right angles (90° angles).

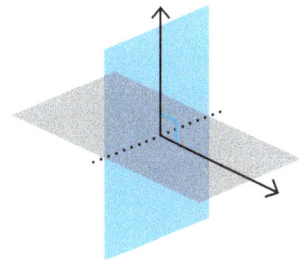

PI π

Symbol used to represent the ratio of the circumference of a circle to its diameter. This ratio is the irrational number 3.1415926....

The most commonly used approximations for pi are 3.14 and $\frac{22}{7}$.

(See CIRCLE, CIRCUMFERENCE, DIAMETER)

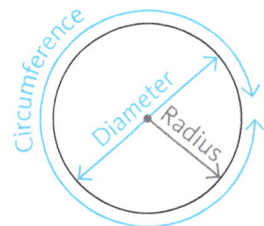

$$\frac{\text{Circumference}}{\text{Diameter}} = \pi = 3.14159...$$

PICTOGRAM

(See PICTOGRAPH)

PICTOGRAPH

A graph or table that uses pictures or symbols to represent data. In a pictograph, each picture or symbol is used to represent a specified quantity, so pictographs are used to display categorical data.

Example: A pictograph showing the number of pears sold at a stand during a 5 month timespan.

Month	Pears sold
June	🍐🍐
July	🍐🍐🍐🍐
August	🍐🍐🍐🍐🍐
September	🍐🍐🍐🍐🍐
October	🍐🍐

🍐 = 20 pears   🍐 = 10 pears

PIE CHART

A circular graph divided into sectors by radii in such a way that the area of each sector represents the percent of the data that is proportional to the quantity of the data it represents. Circle graphs are used to display categorical data.

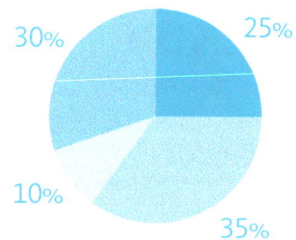

Note: Total data represented in a pie chart is always 100%.

(See CIRCLE GRAPH, GRAPH)

PINT

A unit of measurement of capacity in the customary system.

2 cups = 1 pint
2 pints = 1 quart

(See CAPACITY)

PLACE VALUE
The value of a digit determined by its position within a number.

The value of a digit depends on where it is placed within a number. Each place in a number has a specified value, such as the units position, the tens position, the hundreds position, etc. Place value is the value given to each place or position.

Example: In the decimal or base 10 number system, the place value for 4 in the number 456 is 100; the place value for 5 is 10; the place value for 6 is 1.
$$456 = 4 \times 100 + 5 \times 10 + 6 \times 1$$

Hundreds 10^2	Tens 10^1	Ones 10^0
4	5	6

(See BASE, DECIMAL NUMBER SYSTEM)

PLANE
A flat, two-dimensional surface that extends in all directions to infinity.
A plane surface has length and width but has no thickness or depth.

A plane is flat. Imagine that.
There's nothing thick about it!
A table top; a floor to mop;
A belly-flop! So shout it:
"A plane is flat and only that,
No up, no down!" You know it.
No raiding of the space above
Nor any space below it.

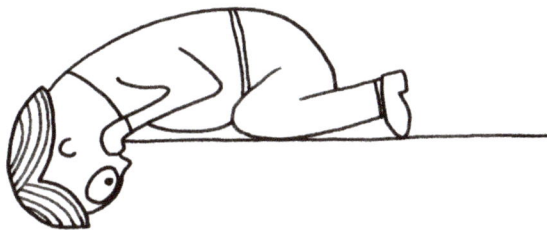

(See DIMENSION)

PLANE FIGURE

A geometric shape that has no thickness and lies entirely in one plane. Plane figures are two dimensional, having length and width but no depth or thickness.

Examples: Squares and circles are plane figures. Any polygon is a plane figure.

(See DIMENSION, PLANE)

PLANE GEOMETRY

The study of lines, angles and shapes in a plane (flat shapes).

(See GEOMETRY)

PLATONIC SOLIDS

Five special polyhedra in which every face is a regular polygon of the same size and shape.

A polyhedron is a solid with flat faces. The Platonic Solids are called regular polyhedra because they are made up of faces that are all the same. They are named after Plato (circa 427-347 BC), a famous Greek philosopher and mathematician, because they were known at this time.

Tetrahedron	Cube	Octahedron	Dodecahedron	Icosahedron
4 triangular faces	*6 square faces*	*8 triangular faces*	*12 pentagonal faces*	*20 triangular faces*

POINT

A point is an exact position or location. It is important to understand that a point is not a thing, but only a place and has no size.

Points are usually named by using a single, upper case letter.

POLAR COORDINATES

A coordinate system used to pinpoint a location on a map or a graph by giving the distance (r) of the location from a point called the origin, and the angle between the axis and a line from the origin to the location.

In this example the distance from the origin is 12 and the angle is 25°.

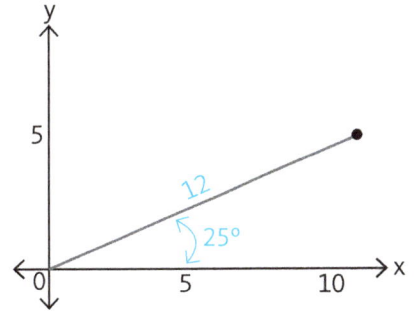

(See COORDINATES)

POLYGON

A two-dimensional shape (a flat shape in a plane) that has only straight sides. If any part of the perimeter of a shape is not a straight line, the shape is not a polygon.

Examples: Triangles, rectangles and pentagons are polygons.

(See CONCAVE, IRREGULAR POLYGON, REGULAR POLYGON)

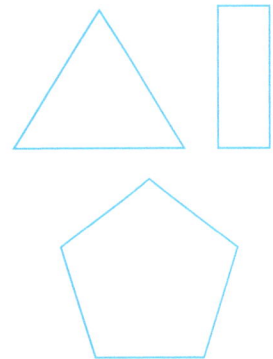

POLYGONAL NUMBERS

A number that can be represented by a regular geometric arrangement of equally spaced points.

Examples: A triangular number is a polygonal number that can be represented by a triangle of points.

Square numbers can be represented by a square of points.

Pentagonal numbers can be represented by a pentagon of points.

(*See FIGURATE NUMBERS*)

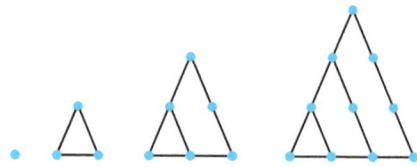
Triangular numbers 1, 3, 6, 10

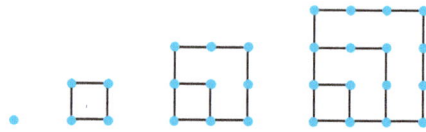
Square numbers 1, 4, 9, 16

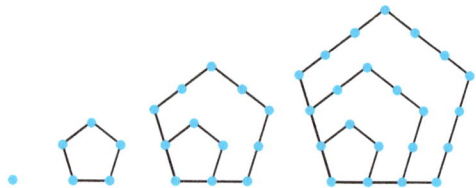
Pentagonal numbers 1, 5, 12, 22

POLYHEDRON

A solid figure bounded by four or more plane faces which are all polygons. The plane (flat) faces of a polyhedron meet along an edge, and three or more edges meet at a point called a vertex. The name is taken from the Greek poly, which means "many", and hedra which means "face". Many polyhedrons are named according to the number of faces they have, such as tetrahedron, dodecahedron, icosahedron, etc.

Examples: In regular polyhedrons all the faces are identical regular polygons and they form equal angles with each other

Polyhedrons that do not have all faces and all angles equal are called irregular polyhedrons.

(*See EDGE, POLYGON, VERTEX*)

Regular polyhedrons

Irregular polyhedrons

POLYNOMIAL

An algebraic expression with two or more terms. The expression can contain constants, variables and exponents.

Examples: $1 + ab$ $2X + Y$ $a^2 + b^2 + c^2$

POPULATION

A selected group of people or objects to be studied for a survey; the group from which a sample is taken.

POSITIVE INTEGER

Any integer that is greater than zero.

POSITIVE NUMBER

A number that is greater than zero. Note that negative means less than zero and that zero is not negative or positive.

On the number line, positive numbers are customarily written right of zero. This is customarily considered the positive direction.

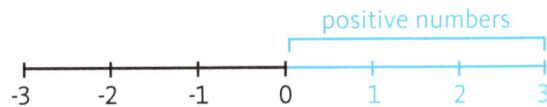

POUND

A unit of weight in the customary system of measurement. Pound is abbreviated as lb.

1 pound = 16 ounces

POWER

A way of saying and writing the same number multiplied by itself several times. The power of a number shows you how many times to use the number as a factor in multiplication. Power is written to the right and above the base number.

Examples: 3^2 means that the base number 3 is used as a factor two times or 3×3; 2^3 means that the base 2 is used as a factor three times or $2 \times 2 \times 2$; n^b means that the number n is used as a factor **b** times or $n \times n \times n...b$ times.

(See BASE, EXPONENT)

PRECISION

The accuracy of a measurement or a calculation. Precision tells us how close a measured value is to the actual value.

PRIME FACTORS

Prime numbers that are factors of a given number.

A prime number that will exactly divide a given number is a prime factor of that number. These prime factors, when multiplied together, give the original number.

Examples: 2 and 3 are the prime factors of 6: $2 \times 3 = 6$
2, 3 and 5 are the prime factors of 30: $2 \times 3 \times 5 = 30$
$4 \times 3 = 12$, but 4 is not a prime factor of 12 because 4 is not a prime number.

(See FACTOR)

PRIME FACTORIZATION

The expression of a whole number as the product of its prime factors.

Example: The prime factorization of 12 is 2 × 2 × 3 or 2^2 × 3.

You can use a factor tree to determine the prime factorization of a whole number.

(See FACTOR TREE)

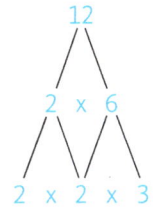

12

2 x 6

2 x 2 x 3

PRIME NUMBER

A natural number whose only factors are 1 and itself. A prime number is a whole number greater than 1 that can be divided evenly only by 1 and itself.

Examples: 3, 5, 7, 11 are all prime numbers. 2 is the only even prime number because all other even numbers are divisible by 2.

PRISM

A three dimensional figure that has two parallel polygon bases that are exactly the same shape and size. The shape of the identical bases give the prism a name.

Examples: A triangular prism has bases that are identical triangles. A rectangular prism has bases that are identical rectangles.

A triangular prism

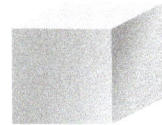

A cube is a rectangular prism

PROPER FACTORS

All the factors of a number, except the number itself and the number 1.

Example: The proper factors of 6 are 2 and 3. The proper factors of 12 are 2, 3, 4, and 6.

(See FACTORS)

PROPER FRACTIONS

Fractions with a value of less than one, meaning a fraction in which the numerator is less than the denominator.

Examples: $\frac{1}{2}, \frac{2}{3}, \frac{3}{4}$ and $\frac{77}{88}$ are all proper fractions.

(See IMPROPER FRACTIONS)

PROBABILITY

The likelihood that something is going to happen.

Probability is often expressed as a fraction between 0 and 1. Using this method, the probability that a particular event (M) will occur out of a total of all possible events that might occur (N) is written as $\frac{M}{N}$. That is:

Probability = $\dfrac{\text{number of times a specified outcome can occur}}{\text{number of all possible outcomes}}$

Note: If something is certain, meaning that out of all possible events (N), all the events will definitely happen, the probability is written as $\frac{N}{N}$; so if something is certain it has a probability of 1. If something is impossible, it has a probability of 0 because out of all possible events, none will happen ($\frac{0}{N}$).

Example: When tossing a coin, the chance of getting heads is 1 chance out of 2 possible outcomes. So the probability of getting heads is $\frac{1}{2}$. The chance of getting tails is the same, or $\frac{1}{2}$. The chance of any other outcome is $\frac{0}{2}$ or 0; the chance of getting either heads or tails is $\frac{2}{2}$ or 1.

PROBLEM

A mathematical situation, usually presented in word form and with a real world context, which requires a solution.

Note: Many of the exercises presented in elementary mathematics textbooks are routine exercises that immediately follow the presentation of a skill or process and are only a practice of the skill; they do not fit the proper definition of problems.

Examples: 3 × 8 requires a solution and is a routine multiplication exercise. Problems are often in written form: John needs $20 to buy a ticket and he has only $18. How many more dollars must he earn?

PRODUCT

The result obtained when multiplying numbers.

Example: 3 × 8 = 24   24 is called the product.

(See MULTIPLICATION)

PROFIT

Income after all expenses have been deducted.

Example: Jake's Lawn Care had an income of $5000 in July. After Jake paid his helper $1500, paid $280 for gas for his truck and mower, paid his office expenses of $150, paid the loan on his equipment of $200 and paid his taxes and medical insurance of $1050, Jake had a profit of $1820.

PROOF

A set of logical arguments used to prove a mathematical theorem from a set of axioms or previously proved theorems.

PROPERTY OF EQUALITY

A rule of algebra that allows us to manipulate, and solve equations. The properties of equality are:

Addition Property of Equality: Adding the same value to both sides of a true equation or inequality results in a true equation or inequality.

Distributive Property of Equality: For all real numbers a, b, and c, $a(b + c) = ab + ac$.

Division Property of Equality: Dividing both sides of a true equation or inequality by the same value results in a true equation or inequality.

Multiplication Property of Equality: Multiplying both sides of a true equation or inequality by the same factor results in a true equation or inequality.

Reflexive Property of Equality: For all real numbers n, $n = n$. That is, a number equals itself.

Substitution Property of Equality: For all real numbers a and b, if $a = b$, then b can be substituted for a in any expression.

Subtraction Property of Equality: Subtracting the same quantity from both sides of a true equation or inequality results in a true equation or inequality.

Symmetric Property of Equality: For all real numbers a and b, if $a = b$, then $b = a$. That is that the order of equals does not change equality.

Transitive Property of Equality: For all real numbers a, b, and c, if $a = b$ and $b = c$, then $a = c$. That is two numbers equal to the same number are equal to each other.

PROPORTION

An equation that states that two ratios are equal. Two or more ratios that are equivalent to each other.

Examples: 1 out of 2 is equal to 2 out of 4 and is equal to 3 out of 6 because all are equal to $\frac{1}{2}$. The ratios are the same, so they are in proportion.

Because proportion says that two ratios (or fractions) are equal, they are often used to solve for some missing information. If only one term of the proportion is unknown then its value can be found by solving the proportion.

PROTRACTOR

A device used in Geometry to measure and draw angles.

An instrument for measuring the size of an angle.

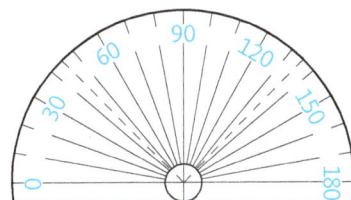

PYRAMID

A polyhedron formed by a polygon and triangles. The polygon is called the base of the pyramid and the triangles are called the faces. The common vertex of these faces is the apex of the pyramid.

Apex

Base

Square pyramid

A pyramid can have any polygon as a base, but Square pyramids, such as the pyramids of Egypt, are most common.

A perpendicular line segment drawn from the apex to the plane of the base is called the altitude of the pyramid. The length of the altitude is called the height of the pyramid.

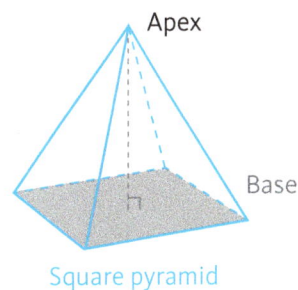

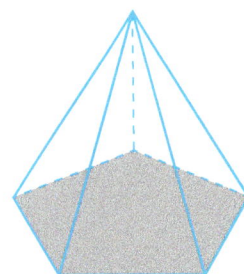

(See POLYHEDRON)

PYTHAGORAS

Greek mathematician and philosopher who lived from c 570 BCE to 495 BCE and is known as Pythagoras of Samos. Pythagoras sought to interpret the entire physical world in terms of numbers and founded their systematic and mystical study; he is best known for the theorem of the right-angled triangle.

Illustration of Pythagoras

PYTHAGOREAN THEOREM

A theorem attributed to Pythagoras that says that the area of the square of the hypotenuse, or the longest side, of a right triangle is equal to the sum of the squares of the other two sides, called the legs. This may sound very difficult at first, but it makes an easy equation.

Here is the theorem again and the equation: The area of the sum of the squares of the lengths of the two shorter sides of a right triangle is equal to the area of the square of the length of the longest side: $c^2 = a^2 + b^2$

In this right triangle the shorter sides, called the legs, are A and B. C is the longer side, called the hypotenuse. The Pythagorean Theorem says that the square of A (A × A) plus the square of B (B × B) is equal to the square of C (C × C): $A^2 + B^2 = C^2$

Example: If A = 3 and B = 4 then: $3^2 + 4^2 = C^2$.
$3^2 = 3 \times 3 = 9$
$4^2 = 4 \times 4 = 16$
$9 + 16 = 25$
$C^2 = 25$ (5 × 5 = 25)   C = 5

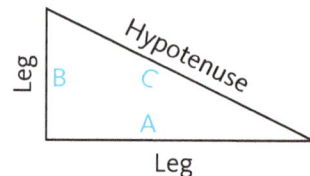

(See RIGHT TRIANGLE)

200

PYTHAGOREAN TRIPLES

Whole numbers that work together in the Pythagorean Theorem. They are also called Pythagorean numbers.

Note: A primitive Pythagorean triple is one in which a, b and c do not share common factors. A right triangle whose sides form a Pythagorean triple is called a Pythagorean triangle.

Examples: Three positive integers, a, b, and c, that do not share common factors and such that $a^2 + b^2 = c^2$ are:

(3, 4, 5)	(5, 12, 13)	(8, 15, 17)	(7, 24, 25)
(20, 21, 29)	(12, 35, 37)	(9, 40, 41)	(28, 45, 53)
(11, 60, 61)	(16, 63, 65)	(33, 56, 65)	(48, 55, 73)
(13, 84, 85)	(36, 77, 85)	(39, 80, 89)	(65, 72, 97)

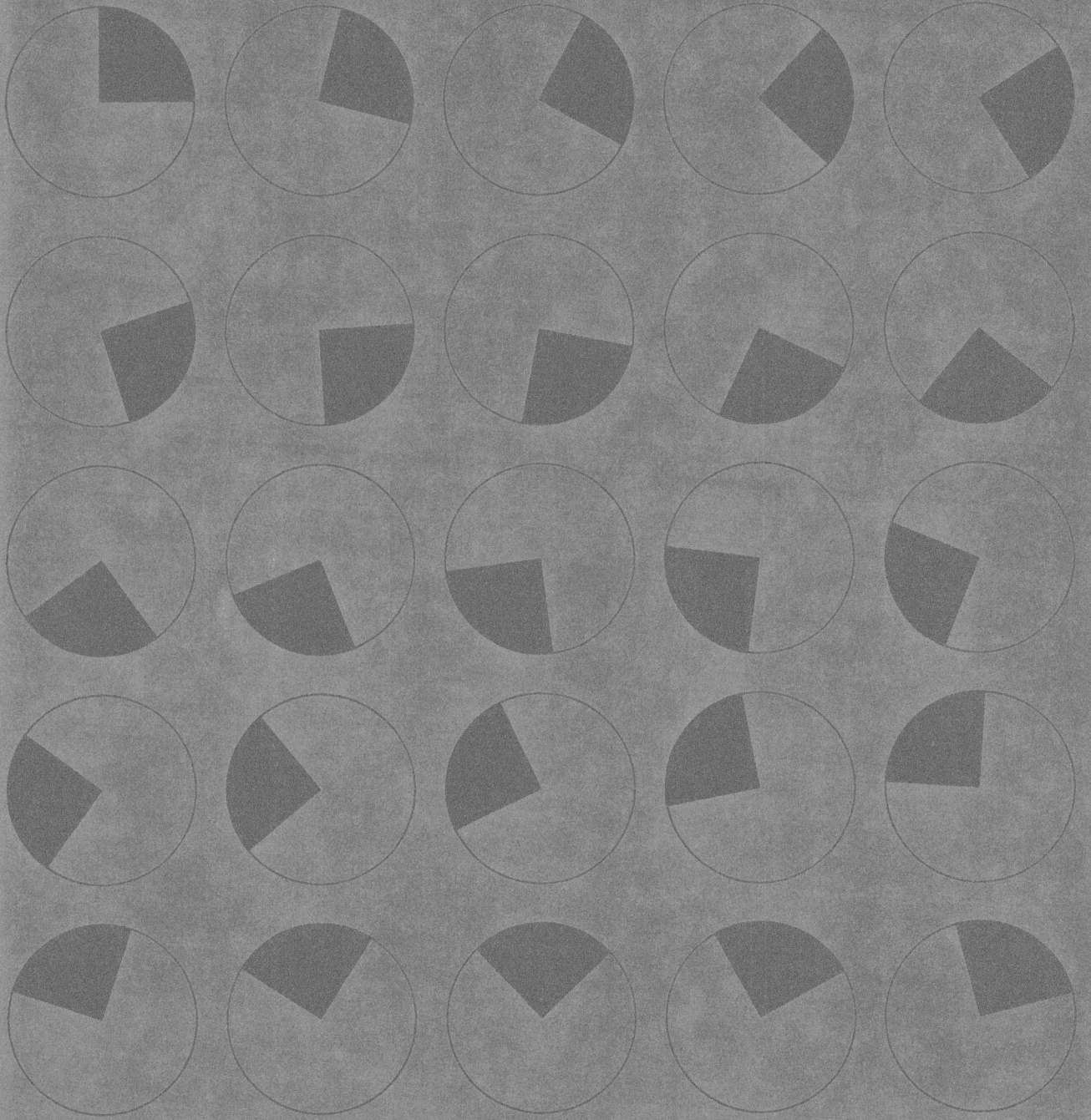

QUADRANT

1) One of the four sections of a rectangular coordinate plane. The quadrants are separated by the axes and are numbered I through IV, beginning at the upper right and moving in a counterclockwise direction.

2) A quarter of a circle formed by any two radiuses that are at right angles to each other and the arc connecting them.

(See CARTESIAN COORDINATE SYSTEM)

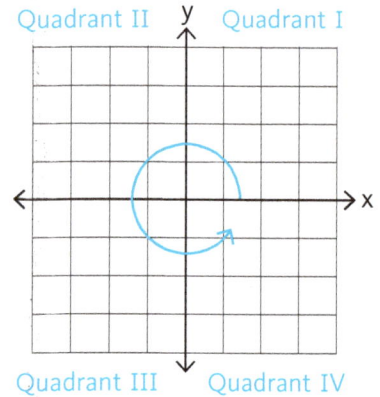

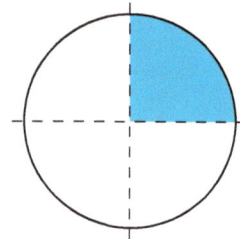

QUADRATIC EQUATION

An equation which has 2 as the highest exponent of the variable. Quadratic equations are usually written $ax^2 + bx + c = 0$ with x as the variable and a, b, c as constants.

Note: The x^2 term makes the equation a quadratic equation. Without an exponential term, it would be a linear equation. Also note that the expression is an equation because it is set equal to 0.

Examples of quadratic equations in the form $ax^2 + bx + c = 0$:
$3x^2 + 2x + 4 = 0$ *(in this equation a = 3, b = 2, c = 15)*
$5x^2 + 15 = 0$ *(in this equation a = 5, b = 0, c = 15)*
$2x^2 + 3x = 0$ *(in this equation a = 2, b = 3, c = 0)*

(See EQUATION, EXPONENT, PAPABOLA, POWER, SQUARE)

QUADRILATERAL

A four sided polygon, meaning a two dimensional shape that has four straight sides.

Examples: Rectangles, kites, trapezoids, rhombi and parallelograms are quadrilaterals.

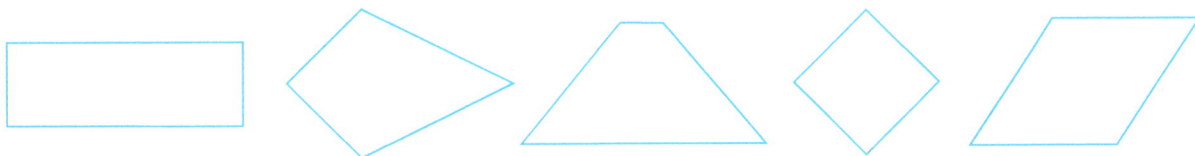

(See POLYGON)

QUADRILLION

One of two different numbers greater than a million, depending on the system used:
1) In the American system, a thousand million millions or a 1 followed by 15 zeros, which can be shown as 1,000 x 1,000,000 x 1,000,000 = 1,000,000,000,000,000 or as 1×10^{15}. It is equal to 1000 trillions.

In this system, the Latin prefix quad refers to the number of groups of three zeros, not including the last group of three zeros, which is a thousand.

Example: In the American system, the Latin prefix bi is used in the number billion and represents **2 groups** of **3 zeros** and one additional group for thousands. A billion is 1,**000,000**,000 or (10^9).

Using this system, a quadrillion is a 1 followed by **4 groups** of **3 zeros** plus an additional 3 zeros for thousands: 1,**000,000,000,000**,000 or (10^{15}).

2) In the British system, the Latin prefix 'quad' represents the exponent or the power of a million. A British quadrillion is 1,000,000,000,000,000,000,000,000 or (10^{24}). This is a much larger number. This system is used much less frequently.

Example: A British billion is (10^{12}) or 1,000,000,000,000.

(See BILLION)

QUART (QT)

A unit of measurement of capacity in the customary system. A quart is equal to 4 cups or 2 pints. There are 4 quarts in 1 gallon.

(See CAPACITY)

QUARTILE

One of the three points that divide a numerically ordered data set into four equal groups, the quartiles mark the 25th, 50th and 75th percentile points. Each group is made up of one quarter of the data. The first quartile (Q1) is the number in the middle between the smallest number and the median of the ordered data set. The second quartile (Q2) is the number that is the median of the data. The third quartile (Q3) is the middle number between the median and the highest value of the data set. Quartiles are used to give us some idea of the spread of data.

Example: Our school is ranked in the first quartile.

(See MEDIAN)

QUANTITATIVE DATA

Data that can be counted or measured. Data that can be counted is called discrete data and data that can be measured is called continuous.

QUANTITY

The amount or number of something. Quantity tells you how much there is of something.

QUARTER

1) One of four equal parts of a whole. The fraction written as $\frac{1}{4}$ signifies 1 of four equal parts.

2) A coin with a value of $\frac{1}{4}$ of a US dollar. A quarter is worth 25 cents and is written 25¢ or $0.25.

This rectangle has been divided into quarters

QUARTER HOUR

A unit of measurement of time that is equal to $\frac{1}{4}$ of an hour. It is equivalent to fifteen minutes.

QUOTATIVE DIVISION

Quotative division determines the number of groups that result when a number is divided into equal groups. Quotative division is sometimes referred to as repeated subtraction or measurement.

Example: There are 24 candies. Three candies must go into each goodie bag. How many goodie bags can be made?

$24 \div 3 = 8$

(See ARRAY, DIVISION)

An array of 24 candies partitioned distributed among 8 bags, each containing 3.

QUOTIENT

The result obtained from the operation of division.

Example: $12 \div 3 = 4$ In a division problem, the quotient is the answer. 4 is the quotient of 12 divided by 3. 12 is the dividend and 3 is the divisor.

HA AH

OMIIMO

UT TU

WV VW

YX XY

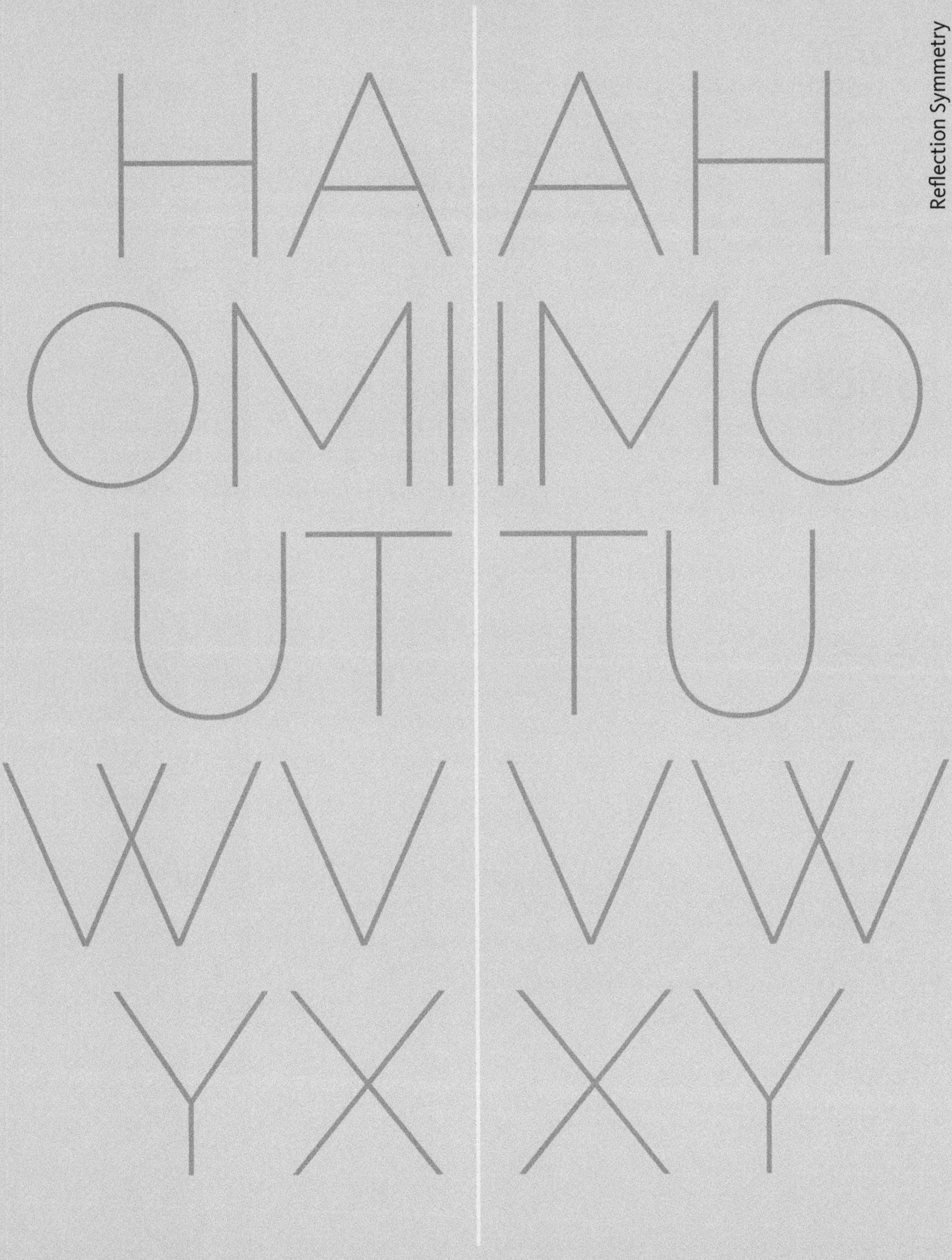

RADIAN

A unit used to measure angles. One radian is the measure of a central angle of a circle that has sides which cut off an arc on the circumference of the circle equal in length to the radius. Using radians over degrees helps to simplify many trigonometric formulas, so you will begin using radians in trigonometry.

(See CIRCLE, DEGREE, TRIGONOMETRY)

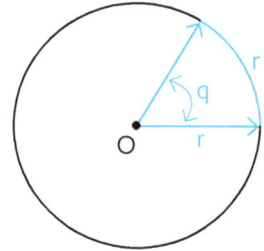

1 radian = q

RADICAL

A symbol used to signify the root of a number. Radicals or roots are the opposite operation of applying exponents; you reverse a power of a number with a radical. When using the square root of a number, the symbol $\sqrt{\ }$ is used to represent the square root of the number written under the radical sign.

Other roots, such as the cube root, are shown by a number written over the radical symbol.

Note that the number under the root symbol is called radicand.

Examples: $\sqrt{4} = 2$ because $2^2 = 4$ $\sqrt{9} = 3$ because $3^2 = 9$

(See EXPONENT, POWER, ROOT)

RADIUS

1) The distance from the center of a circle to any point on its circumference.

2) The distance from the center of a sphere to any point on its surface.

The plural of radius is radii.

(See CIRCLE, SPHERE)

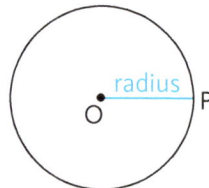

radius

OP is a radius of the circle

OP is a radius of the sphere

RAISE

To multiply a number by itself a given number of times.

Examples: 5 raised to the power of 4 is written as 5^4; $5^4 = 5 \times 5 \times 5 \times 5 = 625$.
3 raised to the power of 5 is written as 3^5. $3^5 = 3 \times 3 \times 3 \times 3 \times 3 = 243$.
Any number, n, raised to the power of 3 is written as n^3; $n^3 = n \times n \times n$.

(See POWER)

RANDOM

An event that occurs without any control on the outcome. When events are random, every event has an equal chance of happening and the result is not predictable. Random events won't follow any pattern or order.

Example: When a fair die is tossed, each of the 6 numbers on its faces is equally likely to occur, so the outcome is random.

RANDOM SAMPLE

Choosing a sample from a population purely by chance, with no predictability. If a sample is random, every member of a population has an equal chance of being selected.

RANGE

The difference between the greatest number and the least number in a set of data. To find the range of a set of data, subtract the smallest number from the largest number.

Range is also used to name **1)** the set of all possible values for the output of a function; and **2)** the set of all of the second coordinates of the ordered pairs.

(See FUNCTION, MEASURE OF VARIATION, ORDERED PAIRS)

RATE

1) A ratio comparing two quantities that are measured in different units.

Example: The speed racer drove 24 laps in 3 minutes.

2) The percentage of interest used when calculating interest payments.

Example: Simple interest is determined by finding the product of the interest rate, principal and time.

RATIO

The relationship in quantity, in amount, or in size between two or more things. A ratio compares values and shows the relative sizes of two or more values, telling how much or how many of one thing exists when compared to another thing. The number of one part of a ratio depends on the other value.

Example: If, in a set of butterflies, ten butterflies are red and twelve are black, then the ratio of red butterflies to black butterflies is 10 to 12. This is the equivalent ratio of 5 to 6.

Ratios are written in different ways:

Using a colon to separate values	Examples: $10 : 12$ or $A : B$
Using the word 'to'	Examples: 10 to 12 or A to B
Using fractional notation	Examples: $\frac{10}{12}$ or $\frac{A}{B}$

Note: If one term of a ratio is zero, this number must be the numerator or the number above the fraction bar.

Example: in $\frac{A}{B}$, $B \neq 0$

Also, it is important to note that, in the expression 'the ratio of red butterflies to black butterflies', red was stated first. In ratios, order is very important and must be maintained. Whichever word is first, the number for that word must also come first. If the expression had been 'the ratio of black to red', then the numbers in the ratio would have to be 12 to 10, varying according to the order in which the elements of the ratio were expressed.

continued ⟶

Examples: If, in a set of buttons, five are round and seven are square, then the ratio of round buttons to square buttons is 5 to 7. The ratio of square buttons to round buttons is 7 to 5.

If you travel 120 miles in 3 hours, that is a ratio of ($\frac{120}{3}$). This is the equivalent ratio of 40 miles in 1 hour ($\frac{40}{1}$).

RATIONAL NUMBER

A number that can be expressed as one integer divided by another integer. All rational numbers can be written as common fractions with integers as both the numerator and the denominator. The set of rational numbers includes the counting numbers, negative numbers, terminating decimals and repeating decimals.

Examples: 4 ($\frac{4}{1}$); $\frac{2}{3}$; and .5 are rational numbers. The square root of 2, (1.41421... a number with a non-repeating decimal), is not a rational number.

(See NUMBER)

RAY

A straight line that originates at a point and extends in only one direction. A ray extends infinitely in one direction from one endpoint.

P •————————→

A ray with its origin at P

REAL NUMBERS

The set of numbers that includes all rational and irrational numbers. All the numbers which can be expressed as decimals are real numbers. The numbers we use to count, positive numbers, negative numbers, fractions, decimals, even irrational numbers are real numbers.

(See IMAGINARY NUMBER)

RECIPROCAL

A number related to another number in such a way that the product of the two numbers is 1.

Examples: The reciprocal of 2 is $\frac{1}{2}$; $2 \times \frac{1}{2} = 1$.

The reciprocal of $\frac{3}{4}$ is $\frac{4}{3}$; $\frac{3}{4} \times \frac{4}{3} = 1$.

To find the reciprocal of a number, divide 1 by the number.

Note that every number has a reciprocal except 0. 0 has no reciprocal because there is no number, n, such that $n \times 0 = 1$.

RECTANGLE

A 4-sided polygon with opposite sides that are parallel and equal in length. In this two-dimensional (flat) shape, the four sides are formed by two pairs of parallel lines crossing each other at right angles. All interior angles of a rectangle are right angles (90°).

(See POLYGON)

Rectangle

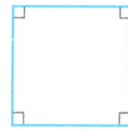

A square is a special rectangle with 4 equal sides

RECTANGULAR COORDINATE SYSTEM

A system with two (for two dimensions) or three (for three dimensions) mutually perpendicular lines (called coordinate axes) and their point of intersection (called the origin) as the frame of reference. Specific locations are described by ordered pairs or triples (called coordinates) that indicate distance from the origin along lines that are parallel to the coordinate axes.

(See CARTESIAN COORDINATE SYSTEM)

RECTANGULAR PRISM

A solid (3-dimensional) object with six faces that are rectangles. A rectangular prism has parallel congruent rectangles as its bases.

(See PRISM)

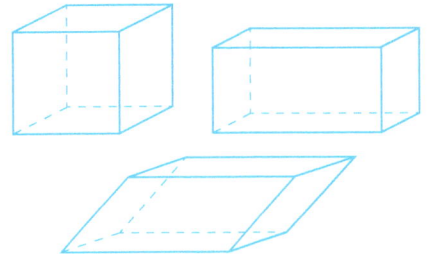

RECURRING DECIMAL

A decimal fraction that repeats one number or a group of numbers after the decimal point without ending. In a recurring decimal, a digit or a pattern of digits repeat forever.

Examples: $\frac{1}{3} = .333333.....$ $\frac{1}{7} = 0.142857142857142857...$

REFLECTION

The mirror image of a figure. A reflection is a transformation in which the new figure is the mirror image of the other. It is also called flip.

(See TRANSFORMATION)

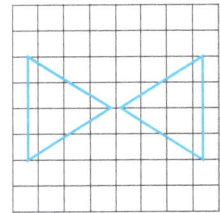

A reflection on a grid

REFLECTION SYMMETRY

Symmetry in which one half of a shape is the reflection of the other half. When a plane shape can be divided into two congruent parts that are mirror images of each other (when you can fold it in half along some axis and have both halves match exactly), it has reflection symmetry.

(See SYMMETRY)

Some letters of the alphabet have reflection symmetry

REFLEX ANGLE

An angle that measures more than 180°
but less than 360°.

(See ANGLE)

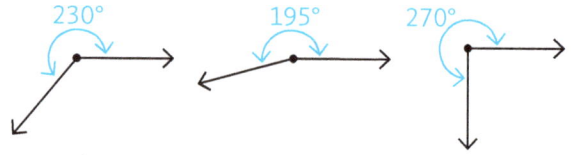

REGROUP

To decompose or compose numbers to form quantities that are compatible for the
arithmetic operations of addition or subtraction.

Regrouping is the process that many remember as 'carrying' or 'borrowing'.

Examples: Regrouping in addition 23 + 48 = 71
In this operation the first column of addends is 3 + 8 = 11, so the
sum of the units position is actually one ten and one unit. In order to
write the 10 in the tens position of the final sum, we must decompose
11 into 1 ten and one unit and add the ten to the tens position. To do
this we add the 10 to the 2 tens and 4 tens of the addends.

$$\begin{array}{r} \overset{tens\ units}{} \\ 1 \\ 23 \\ +\ 48 \\ \hline 71 \end{array}$$

Regrouping in subtraction 52 - 27 = 25
In this operation the first column presents us with 2 - 7, so the
difference of the units position cannot be computed within the
positive integers. In order to complete the subtraction, we must
increase the number in the units position of the minuend. To do
this, we decompose 52 into 4 tens and 12 units. We now subtract
7 from 12. 12 − 7 = 5.

$$\begin{array}{r} \overset{tens\ units}{} \\ 1 \\ 52 \\ -\ 27 \\ \hline 25 \end{array}$$

REGULAR POLYGON

A polygon with all sides the same length and all interior angles equal.

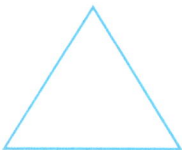  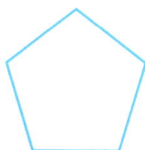  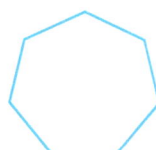 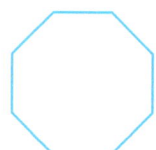

Triangle   Quadrangle   Pentagon   Hexagon   Heptagon   Octagon

(See POLYGON)

REGULAR POLYHEDRON

A polyhedron with faces that are all identical regular polygons and all vertices that have the same number of edges. There are five convex regular polyhedra, known as the Platonic Solids: the tetrahedron, the cube, the octahedron, the dodecahedron and the icosahedron.

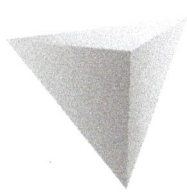    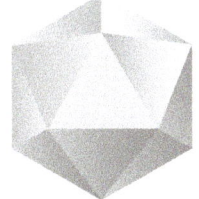

| Tetrahedron | Cube | Octahedron | Dodecahedron | Icosahedron |

(See PLATONIC SOLIDS, POLYHEDRON)

RELATED FACTS

Basic facts of arithmetic operations that form fact families. These facts are created by applying the commutative property and using inverse operations. Related facts can be learned in groups and facilitate learning.

Examples: Given the basic fact 8 + 3 = 11, apply the commutative property for addition to yield the related fact 3 + 8 = 11. Because addition and subtraction are inverse operations the related subtraction facts would be 11 − 3 = 8 and 11- 8 = 3. 8 + 3 = 11, 3 + 8 = 11, 11 − 3 = 8 and 11- 8 = 3 are thus related facts.

Given the basic fact 7 × 3 = 21, apply the commutative property for multiplication to yield the related fact 3 × 7 = 21. Because multiplication and division are inverse operations, the related division facts are 21 ÷ 7 = 3 and 21 ÷ 3 = 7. 7 × 3 = 21, 3 × 7 = 21, 21 ÷ 7 = 3 and 21 ÷ 3 = 7 are related facts.

(See COMMUTATIVE PROPERTY)

RELATION

A collection of ordered pairs in the form (x,y) in which the value of x could have many different values for y.

Example: Ordered pairs are used to locate points in a coordinate system.

(See FUNCTION)

RELATIVE FREQUENCY

The number of times a specific outcome occurs compared to the total number of occurrences of all possible outcomes.

Example: You and a friend play a game 10 times. You win 7 times. The frequency of your winning is 7. The relative frequency is 7 out of 10 or $\frac{7}{10}$. Relative frequency tells you that you have won 70% of the time.

RELATIVELY PRIME

Two numbers are relatively prime if they have no common factors other than the number 1. Numbers that are relatively prime have a greatest common divisor of 1.

Example: 8 and 9 are relatively prime.

(See PRIME NUMBERS)

REMAINDER

Any amount left over after a division.

Example: 28 cannot be evenly divided by 8. 28 ÷ 8 = 3 with a remainder of 4.

REPEATING DECIMAL

(See RECURRING DECIMAL)

REVOLUTION

A 360° angle or one full rotation about a point.

We often see word used in the phrase "Revolutions Per Minute", or "RPM". This tells us how many complete turns occur every minute.

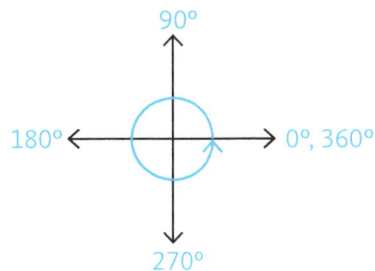

RHOMBUS

A 4-sided polygon with straight sides of equal length. A rhombus is a type of parallelogram, but in a rhombus the opposite sides are not only parallel, they are equal. The opposite angles are also equal. Plural: rhombi.

Note: In common usage, rhombi are often called diamonds. A baseball diamond is a rhombus.

(See POLYGON)

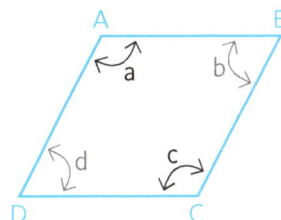

Sides AB, BC, CD, DA are equal.
Angles a and c are equal.
Angles b and d are equal.

RIGHT ANGLE

An angle which measures 90° or one fourth of a full revolution.

Note: The symbol we use to show that an angle is a right angle is a little square drawn at the intersection of the lines forming the angle.

Example: The 4 angles of a square are right angles.

(See ANGLE, REVOLUTION)

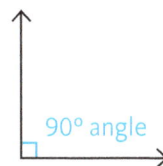

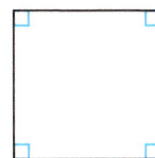

A square has 4 right angles

RIGHT TRIANGLE

A triangle that contains one 90° angle.

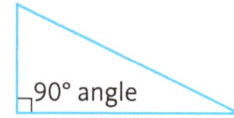
90° angle

RISE

The vertical change between two points on a line as measured in a rectangular coordinate system. The rise tells us just how steep the angle of the line is compared to the x axis. The ratio of rise to run (or the horizontal change between the two points on a line) gives the gradient or slope of the line.

(*See RECTANGULAR COORDINATE SYSTEM, RUN*)

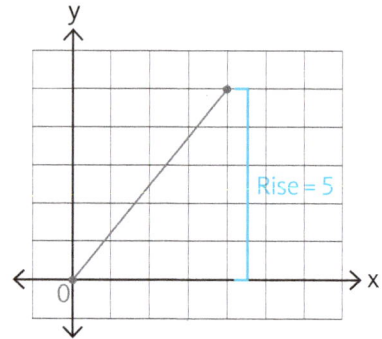
Rise = 5

ROMAN NUMERALS

The numerals of an ancient European number system. The seven symbols for Roman numerals are: I which represents 1, V (5), X (10), L (50), C (100), D (500) and M (1000). The system is not a place value system as we use it, and there is no value for zero in the system.

In this system, numbers are found by adding or subtracting the values of the individual symbols depending on their location in the number. When a Roman symbol is followed by one of less value, the represented quantity is obtained by adding the values of individual symbols. When a symbol of less value is written before a symbol of greater value, the represented quantity is obtained by subtracting the values of individual symbols.

Examples: V I = V (or 5) + I (or 1) = 6
         I V = V (or 5) - I (or 1) = 4

ROOT OF AN EQUATION

The values of a variable in an equation that make the equation true.

Example: In the equation $x^2 = 4$, there are two values that make the equation true. If $x = 2$ the equation is true; if $x = -2$ the equation is true. The roots of the equation are 2 and -2.

ROTATION

The turning of a two dimensional figure around a fixed point, or the turning of a three dimensional figure around a fixed axis.

Note: One complete turn is a full rotation of 360°.

(See TRANSFORMATION)

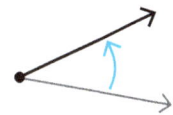

Rotation of a two dimensional figure

ROTATIONAL SYMMETRY

A geometric shape has rotational symmetry about a point if it can be rotated about the point less than one complete turn and its image remains the same.

Turn them about and see! Find other shapes with rotational symmetry.

Snowflake

Some letters of our alphabet have rotational symmetry

Square

ROUNDING

Finding an approximate number with fewer digits to make estimation calculation easier. The result will be less accurate, but is often acceptable because it is easier to use. Usually, numbers are rounded up (to a higher number) or down (to a lower number) to the nearest ones, tens, hundreds....

The most common method of rounding is to first decide to which place you are going to round. Increase the digit in this place by 1 if the digit in the next place is 5 or greater. If the digit in the next place is less than 5, keep the digit the same. Each digit after the place to which you are rounding always becomes zero.

Examples: Round 3.979876 to the hundredths place. The digit in the thousandths place is 9, so we increase the digit in the hundredths place to 8. All digits after the hundredths place become zeros. 3.980000 or 3.98

Round 2891 to the nearest tens (or tens place). The digit in the ones place is 1, so we leave the digit in the tens place the same. All digits after the tens place become zeros. 2890

Round 2891 to the nearest hundreds (or hundreds place): 2900

ROW

Numbers or items in a horizontal line. An arrangement of numbers or items horizontally from left to right in an array or a horizontal line of numbers in a matrix.

Note: Items arranged in a column are vertical or downward.

(See ARRAY, MATRIX, TABLE)

RUN

The horizontal change between two points on a line. The run is equal to the difference between the points on the x axis in a rectangular coordinate system. The ratio of rise to run gives the gradient or slope of the line that passes through the two points.

(See RECTANGULAR COORDINATE SYSTEM, RISE)

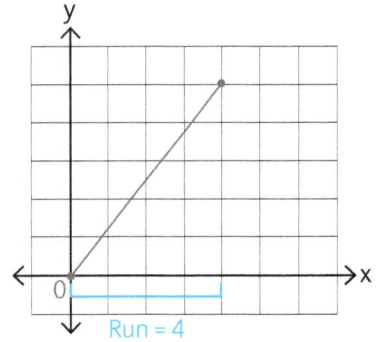

Run = 4

SAMPLE

A smaller selection taken from a larger group. A sample selected to represent a larger set or population allows us to examine attributes of the larger group.

Example: Inspectors carefully examined a sample of the toys produced in the factory to determine their safety.

SCALAR

A quantity, which has only size but no direction. A scalar is a number as distinguished from a vector.

Example: Volume is a scalar quantity.

(See VECTOR)

SCALE

1) A series of ordered marks at regular intervals along a line or curve used for measurement.

Example: The marks on a ruler or a protractor.

2) The ratio of the size of objects depicted in a painting, drawing, sculpture or a map compared to the size of the real object.

Note: A model of an actual object that only differs in size is called a scale model. A scale model is usually smaller than the actual object. The ratio between the size of the model and that of the actual object gives the scale of the model.

Example: Each $\frac{1}{8}$ inch on a map could represent a mile.

3) An instrument for weighing or to compare masses.

Example: The scale you see in the grocery store used for weighing fruit and vegetables.

SCALE DRAWING

A drawing that results from enlarging or reducing all of the dimensions of an object by a specified scale factor.

(See SCALE)

SCALE FACTOR

The ratio of the lengths of corresponding sides in similar geometric figures. The scale factor can be interpreted as the number used to multiply each dimension of a figure in order to create a similar figure.

(See SIMILAR FIGURES)

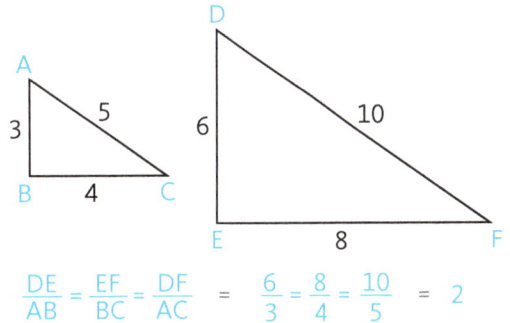

$$\frac{DE}{AB} = \frac{EF}{BC} = \frac{DF}{AC} = \frac{6}{3} = \frac{8}{4} = \frac{10}{5} = 2$$

SCALENE TRIANGLE

A triangle with no two sides having the same length. In a scalene triangle none of the sides or angles are equal.

(See TRIANGLE)

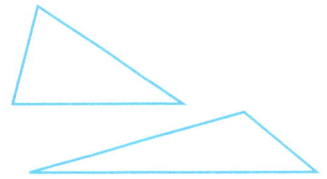

SCATTER PLOT

A graph made by plotting points in a coordinate plane that shows the relationship between two sets of data.

Example: If we used one axis of a coordinate graph to plot the height of a group of people and the other axis to plot their weight, the scatter plot would show the relationship between height and weight for that population.

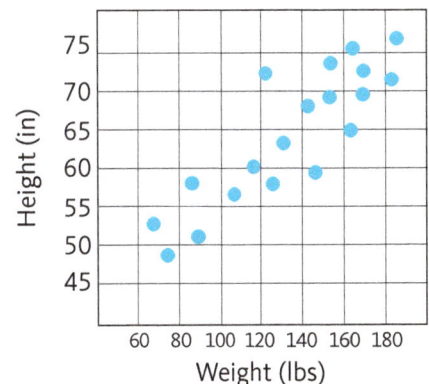

SCIENTIFIC NOTATION

A way to represent a very large or very small number as the product of a number between 1 and 10 and a power of 10.

To rewrite a very large or very small number:

a) Place the decimal point after the first non-zero digit.

Examples: For the number 839.426 you would write 8.39426
For the number 0.0000345 you would write 3.45

b) This number is then raised to the appropriate power of 10, that is to the power of ten that would put the decimal point back where it should be.

Examples: For the number 839.426 you would write 8.39426×10^3
For the number 0.0000345 you would write 3.45×10^{-5}

In scientific notation the speed of light or 299,790,000 m/s would be written as 2.9979×10^8 m/s

---

SECANT

1) A straight line that intersects a curve at two or more points.

A secant of a circle will intersect the circle at only two points.

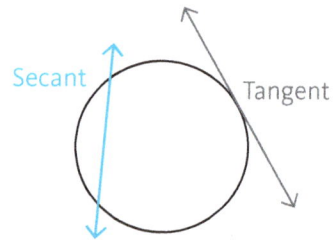

Note: If a straight line only meets one point on a curve it is called a tangent.

2) In the geometry of a right triangle, the secant is the reciprocal of the cosine.

In a right triangle, the length of the hypotenuse divided by the length of the side adjacent to the angle. Secant is usually abbreviated as sec.

SEC = hypotenuse ÷ adjacent.

(See COSINE, TRIGONOMETRY)

SECOND

1) An ordinal number or a number that names the position of something in a list.

Example: Second is the ordinal number that immediately follows the first in a list.

2) A unit for measuring short periods of time.

Example: There are 60 seconds in 1 minute and 3,600 seconds in an hour. One second is about the time of one heartbeat.

3) A unit for measuring angles in a plane.

Example: A second is equal to one-sixtieth of a minute or one three hundred and sixtieth of a degree.

(See ANGLE)

SECTOR

The area of a circle between two radii and their connecting arc.

Minor sector

Major sector

Note: Any two radii will divide a circle into two sectors called a major sector and a minor sector. A minor sector of a circle is sometimes called a wedge.

(See ARC, CIRCLE, RADIUS)

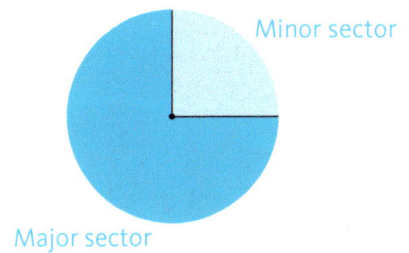

SEGMENT

1) Part of a straight line or a curve that lies between two given points on the line or curve.

2) The area of a circle defined by a straight line that intersects the circle and the enclosed arc. The central angle of a segment of a circle is always less than 180°.

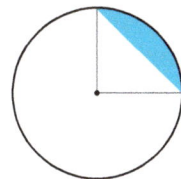

(See CENTRAL ANGLE)

SEMI-
A prefix that means half.

Examples: A semicircle is one half of a circle. Something that occurs semiannually occurs every six months.

SEQUENCE
A set of numbers or objects arranged according to a specific rule or a defined pattern.

Example: 0, 3, 6, 9, 12... is a sequence starting at 0 and increasing by 3 each time.

(See ARITHMETIC SEQUENCE, GEOMETRIC SEQUENCE)

SERIES
The sum of all the terms of a sequence of numbers.

When the limit of a series is a finite number, the series is convergent.

Example: $1 + \frac{1}{2} + \frac{1}{4} + \frac{1}{8}$... is a convergent series.

When the limit of a series is infinite, the series is divergent.

Example: 2 + 4 + 6 + 8... is a divergent series.

(See SEQUENCE)

SET
A collection or group of things selected according to a well-defined rule. Each object or number within the set is called a member or an element of the set. Each element of a set is unique.

Examples: {2, 4, 6, 8} is the set of even numbers less than 10.
Dogs belong to the set of animals with 4 legs, as do cats and cows.

SHAPE

The form or outline of a two-dimensional figure or a three-dimensional object.

Note: The shape of a figure or an object is only its outline. It does not tell us what it is made of or where it is.

Example: A polygon is a two dimensional shape with straight sides. A sphere is a three dimensional shape.

SHARING

A form of division accomplished by splitting into equal parts or shares, also called partition division.

Example: 3 people sharing 9 slices of pizza.

SIDE

A term used in geometry to specify one of the lines that define a two dimensional shape or one of the surfaces of a three dimensional object.

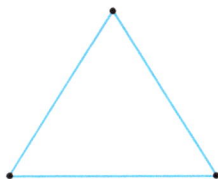

Three line segments form the sides of a triangle

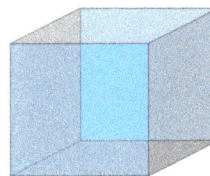

Six squares form the sides of this cube

SIGN

1) A symbol that tells us whether a number is positive (+) or negative (-).

2) A symbol used instead of words.

Examples: % represents percent.
 =, > and < are signs that indicate the relationship between numbers.
+, -, ×, ÷ are symbols that indicate the type of an operation to be carried out on a group of numbers.

SIGNED NUMBER

A number that is specified as being positive or negative.

(See NEGATIVE NUMBER, POSITIVE NUMBER)

SIGNIFICANT DIGITS

In a measurement, the number of digits that are known with some degree of reliability. Most measurements are approximations because no measuring device can give perfect measures. Significant digits are used to indicate how precise a measurement is.

Note: A non-zero digit is always significant. Zeros between non-zero digits are significant. Leading zeros (those that come before the first non-zero number) are not significant digits. Trailing zeros that are to the right of a decimal point are significant because they indicate the level of precision of a measuring device. Trailing zeros to the left of the decimal point may not be significant.

Example: The number 356,000 means that the true value of the measurement might be between 355,500 and 356,500. Therefore, 356,000 has only three significant digits.

SIMILAR FIGURES

Shapes are similar if the only difference between them is their size and/or position. Their corresponding angles will be congruent and their sides will be in exact proportion.

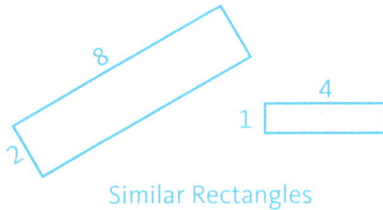

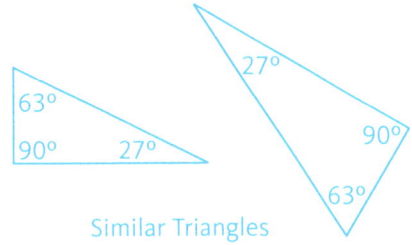

Similar Rectangles

Similar Triangles

SIMILAR TRIANGLES

Triangles with congruent corresponding angles and with sides that are in exact proportion.

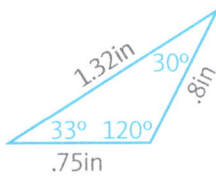

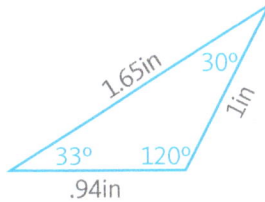

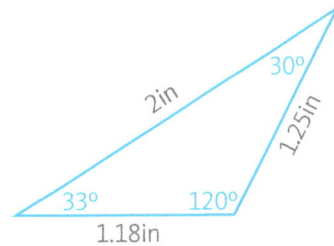

SIMPLE INTEREST

Interest paid on only the principal that was initially invested. Simple interest is computed by multiplying the principal by the rate by the time.

I = PRT   I is the interest, P the principal, R the interest rate, and T the time.

Example: Simple interest on $600 borrowed at 5% for 2 years would be computed as $600 × 5% × 2 = $60.

(See COMPOUND INTEREST)

SIMPLEST FORM

1) A fraction in which the greatest common factor of the numerator and denominator is 1.

Example: $\frac{3}{9}$ is equivalent to $\frac{1}{3}$. This is its simplest form.

2) An expression in algebraic notation that cannot be simplified further.

Example: 3 + (5 × 7) can be written as 3 + 35 or 38.
38 is its simplest form.

(See LOWEST TERMS)

SIMPLIFY

1) To reduce a fraction to its lowest terms.

2) To combine like terms of a mathematical expression.

(See SIMPLEST FORM)

SINE

In a right triangle, the length of the side opposite an angle divided by the length of the hypotenuse. Sine is usually abbreviated as sin.

SIN α = opposite ÷ hypotenuse.

Note: The sine of an angle is a constant because the sides of a right triangle are in proportion depending on the angles.

Example: The sine of angle CAB is the same as the sine of angle CDE.

(See TRIGONOMETRIC FUNCTIONS)

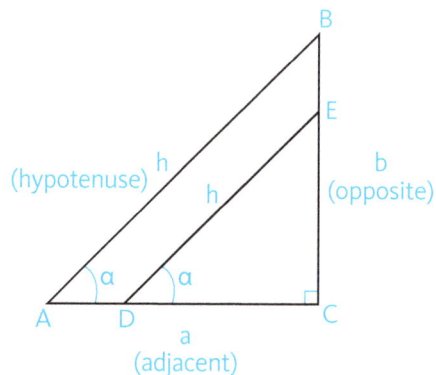

SKEW LINES

Straight lines that are neither parallel nor intersecting because they lie in different planes.

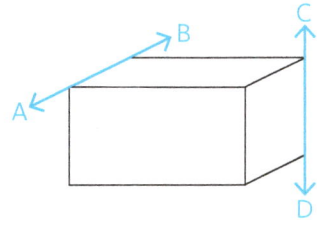

SKEWED DATA

Data that is overweight in one direction. When graphed in a bell shaped curve, skewed data will show a greater concentration on one side or the other of the mean.

(See MEAN, NORMAL DISTRIBUTION)

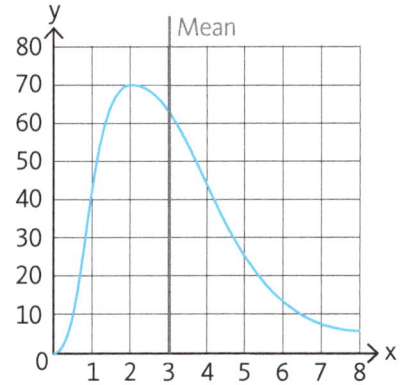

SKIP COUNT

Counting in groups greater than 1.

Examples: Beginning at 0 and skip counting by 2 would be 2, 4, 6, 8, 10...
Beginning at 0 and skip counting by 5 would be 5, 10, 15, 20, 25...

SLIDE

A transformation in which every point of a figure in a plane moves in the same direction by the same distance. Also called a translation, in a slide, the original object and its translation have the same shape and size and maintain the same direction.

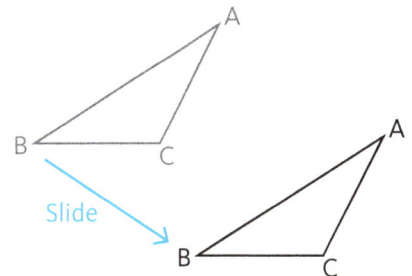

SLOPE

A number that defines how steep a straight line is and whether the line is going up (increasing or in a positive direction) or down (decreasing or in a negative direction). The slope can be defined as the rise over the run.

Note: Rise over run is usually written as a ratio (fraction) of the change on the y axis (the rise) over the corresponding change in the x axis (the run).

(See RISE, RUN)

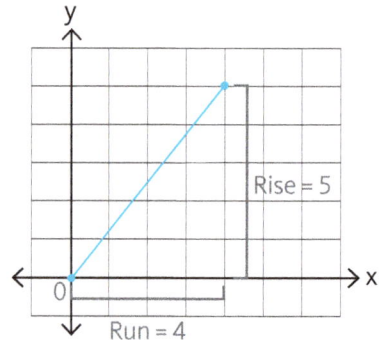

Rise = 5

Run = 4

Slope $= \dfrac{5}{4} = 1.25$

SOLID

A three dimensional object that has width, depth and height. Solids have shape and volume.

Examples: Spheres, cubes, pyramids, cones and cylinders are solid objects.

SOLUTION OF AN EQUATION

The value or set of values that, when substituted for the variable(s), make the equation true.

Examples: $x = 3$ is the solution to the equation $x + 2 = 5$ because $3 + 2 = 5$.

$x = 2$ or $x = -2$ are the solutions to the equation $x^2 - 3 = 1$

$x = 1$ and $y = 3$ is one of many solutions to the $2x + 3y = 11$. Another is $x = 4$ and $y = 1$.

(See EQUATION)

SOLUTION OF AN INEQUALITY

The set of values that, when substituted for the variable(s) in an inequality, make the inequality true.

Examples: Any number which is greater than 3 (x > 3) is the solution to x + 2 > 5

x > -5 and x < 2 describes the set of values that makes |2x + 3| < 7 true.

SPEED

Distance traveled per unit time. Speed tells us how fast something is moving but does not take into account direction, so speed is a scalar quantity. The vector equivalent of speed is velocity.

(See VECTOR, VELOCITY)

SPHERE

A closed solid bounded by a surface with all points an equal distance from a point at its center. If you can imagine rotating a circle around a line that passes through its center, this would give you a sphere.

SPIRAL

A curve which begins at a central point, and then moves further away as it revolves around the point. As the curve of a spiral rotates around and away from the fixed point at its origin it becomes less curved.

Notes: The spiral that can be formed inside a golden rectangle is called the golden spiral. A spiral is sometimes confused with a helix, which is not planar.

(See HELIX, GOLDEN RECTANGLE)

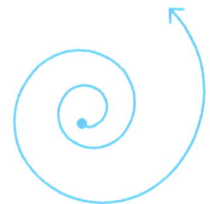

SQUARE

A 4 sided polygon with all 4 sides of equal length, and every interior angle measuring 90°. A square is a regular quadrilateral and a regular polygon.

(See POLYGON, REGULAR POLYGON)

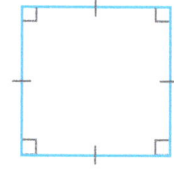

SQUARE NUMBER

Any integer that is also the square of an integer. A square number can be factored into the product of an integer multiplied by itself.

Examples: 1, 4, 9, or 16 are square numbers.

$1 = 1 \times 1 = 1^2$
$4 = 2 \times 2 = 2^2$
$9 = 3 \times 3 = 3^2$
$16 = 4 \times 4 = 4^2$

Square numbers 1, 4, 9, 16

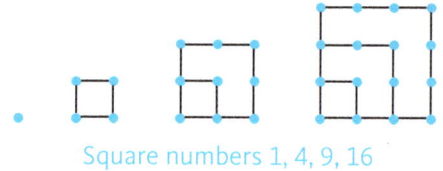

Note: Square numbers are figurate numbers and can be represented in the shape of a square.

SQUARE ROOT

The square root of a number is a value that, when multiplied by itself, gives the number. In other words, the square root of a number, when used as a factor twice, will result in the number.

$\sqrt{16} = 4$ $\sqrt{4} = 2$
Square roots

Example: $4 \times 4 = 16$, so 4 is the square root of 16.

Radical sign

The symbol we use to represent a square root is called a radical sign. The number under the radical sign is called the radicand.

238

SQUARE UNIT
(FOOT, INCH, KILOMETER, MILE, ETC.)
The area of a square that measures 1 unit of length
(1 centimeter, 1 foot, 1 inch, 1 kilometer, 1 mile, etc.)
on each side.

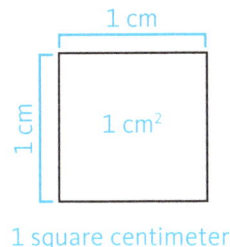

1 square centimeter

STANDARD DEVIATION
The average amount by which the individual items in a set of data are different from the arithmetic mean of all the data in the set. The standard deviation will give you a measure of how spread apart the individual items in a set of data will likely be.

(See ARITHMETIC MEAN, VARIANCE)

STANDARD UNIT
Units of measurement that have a universally accepted value.

Examples: Inch, foot, mile, meter, kilometer, cup, quart, gallon, ounce and pound all have a standard value. Can you think of more?

(See MEASUREMENT)

STATISTICS
A branch of mathematics that studies and interprets data. Statistics involves collecting, organizing, analyzing, interpreting and representing numerical data.

STRAIGHT ANGLE

An angle that measures 180°. A straight angle is the angle formed by half a complete revolution of 360°. It is equal to two right angles.

(See ANGLE)

STRAIGHT LINE

A line that does not curve. A straight line is the shortest distance between two points. In Euclidean geometry a line is always considered to be straight.

(See LINE)

SUBSCRIPT

A small number, letter or symbol written below and to the right of a letter for various purposes.

Examples: The numbers in a sequence may be written by using the same letter for every number and then a subscript to indicate the position of each number within the sequence: a_1, a_2, a_3, ...

Subscripts are used to indicate a number that is not in the base 10, such as binary numbers which are in the base 2.

SUBTRACTION

A mathematical operation to find the difference between two numbers. It is one of the four basic arithmetic operations. The symbol we use to indicate subtraction is the minus sign (-).

Examples: Subtraction is the process you use to find out how many you have left when some are taken away.

If you have 7 plates and break 2, how many remain? 7 - 2 = 5.
This is the take away (or separation) model for subtraction.

I have 7 cookies. Mary has 2 cookies. How many more cookies do I have than Mary? 7 - 2 = 5.
This is the comparison model for subtraction.

I have 7 stamps in my collection. Two stamps are on the first page of my album. The rest are displayed in a frame. How many stamps are in the frame?
This is the part-whole model for subtraction.

SUBTRAHEND

In the arithmetic operation of subtraction, the number that is subtracted.
The components in a subtraction problem are called the minuend, the subtrahend and the difference: minuend – subtrahend = difference

Example: 15 – 7 = 8   In this problem 7 is the subtrahend.

SUM

The quantity resulting from adding two or more numbers together. In the arithmetic operation of addition, the sum is the result.

Example: If you have 7 plates and buy 2 more, how many do you have? Find the sum. 7+ 2 = 9.

SUPPLEMENTARY ANGLES

Two angles that together equal 180°. The angles do not have to be positioned together to be supplementary. The supplement of an angle is another angle that measures the number of degrees needed to make a 180° angle. To find the supplement of an angle less than 180°, subtract the angle from 180°.

Example: Angles that measure 60° and 120° are supplementary angles.

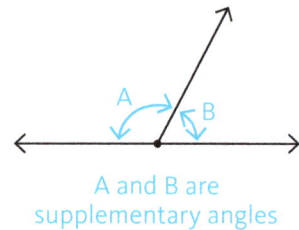

A and B are supplementary angles

SURFACE

A two-dimensional boundary that forms the outside layer of an object.

A surface can be flat, such as the surface of a plane, or curved, such as the surface of a sphere.

SURFACE AREA

The total area of the exterior surface of a solid. If the solid is a polyhedron, the surface area is the sum of the areas of all the faces. If the solid is a sphere the formula for the surface area is $4\pi r^2$, where r is the radius.

(See POLYHEDRON, SOLID)

SURVEY

Gathering information by individual samples to answer questions about a set of data.

Examples: Surveying the members of your class to determine how many have pets and how many of these pets are dogs. Scientists could survey the quality of air in a certain town by taking samples at different times of the day.

(See DATA)

SYMBOL

An image used to represent something instead of using a word or words.

Example: In mathematics, we use symbols to represent the arithmetic operations $(=, -, \times, \div)$ and for number relations: greater than $(>)$, less than $(<)$ and equal $(=)$.

SYMMETRY

A property of a shape or solid composed of congruent parts facing each other across a line, a plane or around an axis. A figure that is symmetric has a balanced arrangement on opposite sides of a line or plane or around a point.

When a line can divide a figure in a plane into two symmetrical parts in such a way that the part of the figure on one side of the line is the mirror image of the part of the figure on the other side we say the figure has line symmetry.

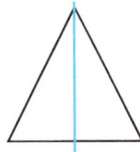

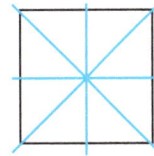

A line of symmetry divides a figure into two congruent parts

A square has 4 lines of symmetry

A geometric shape with rotational symmetry can be rotated about a point less than one complete turn while its image remains the same.

Snowflake

Some letters of our alphabet have rotational symmetry

Square

Solids can have symmetry across a plane.

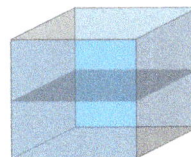

A sphere and a cube can be divided into symmetric parts by a plane.

(See LINE SYMMETRY, ROTATIONAL SYMMETRY)

T

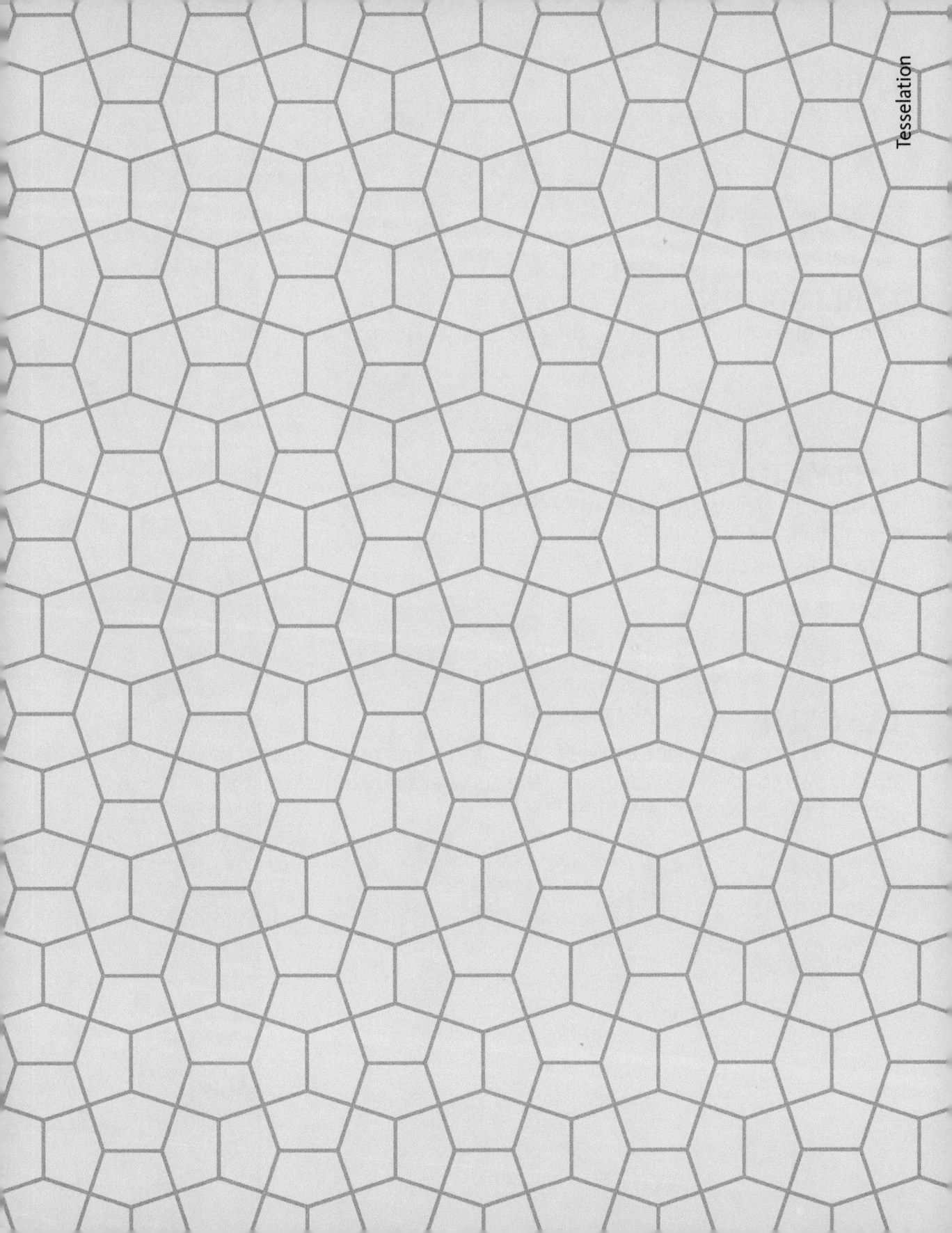

TABLE

Data arranged for visual display in rows and columns.

Example: Table of the pets people in a class have.

(See COLUMNS, DATA, ROW)

Dogs	12
Cats	6
Snakes	2
Gerbils	1
Elephants	0

TABLESPOON

A unit of measure of capacity in the customary system of measurement.

16 tablespoons = 1 cup

TALLY CHART

A chart that displays frequency of an occurrence. A small line, called a tally, is used to record each instance as one count.

(See FREQUENCY TABLE)

Ice Cream	Tally	Frequency
Vanilla	卌 l	6
Chocolate	卌 lll	8
Strawberry	llll	4

Favorite ice cream flavors of children in a kindergarten classroom

TANGENT

A line that intersects a circle at just one point. A line that meets a curve at one point is also considered a tangent to the curve at that point, even though it may intersect the curve at other points.

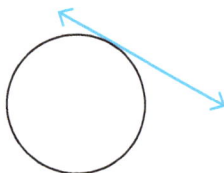

Tangent to a circle

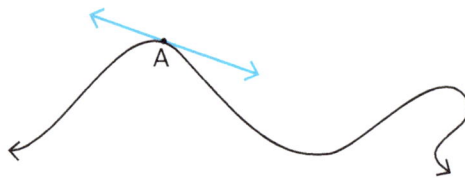

Tangent to a curve at point A

TANGENT OF AN ANGLE

In a right triangle, the length of the side opposite an angle divided by the length of the side adjacent to it. TAN α = opposite ÷ adjacent.

Note: The tangent of an angle is a constant because the sides of a right triangle are in proportion depending on the angles.

(See TRIGONOMETRIC FUNCTIONS)

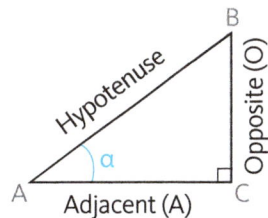

Tangent of angle $\alpha = \dfrac{O}{A}$

TANGRAM

An ancient Chinese puzzle made from a square cut into seven polygon-shaped pieces that can be arranged to make different shapes.

For more tangrams, see another great MathWord Press publication: *Tangram ABC: Shaping the Alphabet from an Ancient Chinese Puzzle.* Available on Amazon.com.

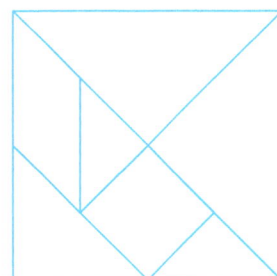

Tangram

Tangram dog

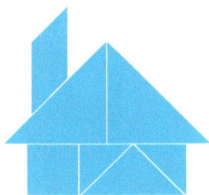

Tangram house

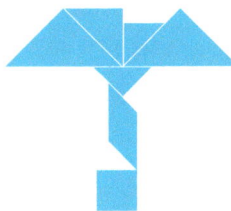

Tangram umbrella

Tangram quail

TAPE DIAGRAM

A linear scale model used to aid mathematics problem solving.

Example: On the opening day of the carnival, a total of 248 tickets were sold. Three times as many children's tickets were sold than adult tickets. How many tickets of each type were sold on opening day.

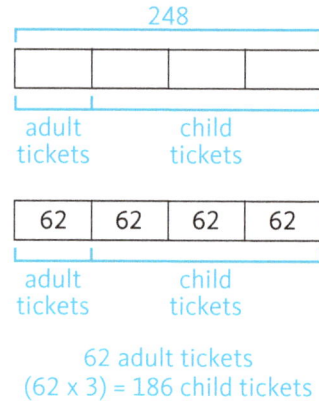

248

adult tickets   child tickets

62	62	62	62

adult tickets   child tickets

62 adult tickets
(62 x 3) = 186 child tickets

TEASPOON

A unit of measure of capacity in the customary system of measurement.

3teaspoons = 1 tablespoon

TEMPERATURE

The degree of heat or cold emanating from an object or substance, or in the atmosphere. Temperature is measured in terms of degrees on a Fahrenheit or Celsius scale, or on the Kelvin scale.

TENTH

One of ten equal parts of a group or unit. One tenth is one of the parts that result from dividing something into ten equal parts. Tenths are the in the first position to the right of the decimal point in the decimal number system.

One tenth is written as the fraction $\frac{1}{10}$ or in decimal notation as 0.1.

Example: 7.2 is read as 7 and 2 tenths.

(See DECIMAL FRACTION, DECIMAL NUMBER SYSTEM)

TERM

A term is a component of a ratio, a proportion, a sequence, an expression, an equation or inequality, or the numerator or denominator of a fraction. The word term is used to signify the parts of an expression separated by + or − signs, or one part of a sequence separated from the others by commas.

Examples: In the expression $3a^2 - 2ab + 3$, $3a^2$, $2ab$, and 3 are terms of the expression. Note: A term such as (ab) can be viewed as both an expression and a term. It is a monomial expression because it consists of only one term.

In the fraction $\frac{a}{xy}$, a and xy are terms.

TERMINATING DECIMAL

A decimal that ends.

Note: Decimal numbers can be recurring (repeating) such as .3333... or 2.123123123...; they can go on forever without ever forming a pattern that repeats such as $\pi = 3.14159...$; or they can terminate.

Note: Zeros can be added to the right of a terminating decimal but do not change its value.

Example: $\frac{1}{2}$ = .5 which is a terminating decimal. $\frac{1}{2}$ can also be written as .50.

TESSELLATION

A repeating pattern of shapes that covers a plane without any overlaps or gaps. Some polygons will tessellate, others will not. A tessellation is often called a tiling. When the shapes used are all regular polygons, the tessellation is called a regular tiling.

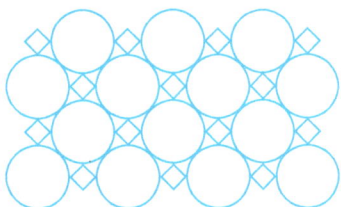

Tessellation or tiling

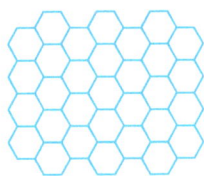

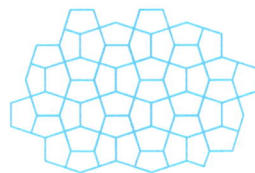

Tessellations or regular tilings

TETRAHEDRON

A polyhedron that has four triangular plane faces. If all four faces of a tetrahedron are congruent equilateral triangles, it is called a regular tetrahedron and is one of the Platonic Solids.

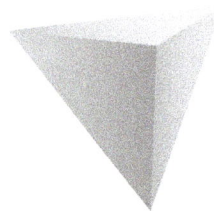

(See PLATONIC SOLIDS, POLYHEDRON)

THEOREM

A mathematical statement that has been proven to be true. A theorem is a conclusion that has been proven by using accepted facts already known and proven.

Examples: Pythagorean Theorem; Fundamental Theorem of Algebra.

THOUSANDTH

One of one thousand equal parts of a group or unit. One thousandth is one of the parts that result from dividing something into one thousand equal parts. Thousandths are the in the third position to the right of the decimal point in the decimal number system.

One thousandth is written as the fraction $\frac{1}{1000}$ or in decimal notation as 0.001.

Examples: 7.002 is read as 7 and 2 thousandths. In the number 46.337, 7 is in the thousandths place.

(See DECIMAL FRACTION, DECIMAL NUMBER SYSTEM)

THREE DIMENSIONAL

Figures that cannot lie in a plane. An object that has height, width and depth, like objects in the real world, is three dimensional. Three dimensional figures are measured in three directions.

Examples: A book and your shoes – and you! – are three dimensional.

(See DIMENSION)

TILING

The process of covering a surface with unit squares to determine the area of a figure.

(See UNIT SQUARE, TESSELATION)

A 3 by 5 tiling with unit squares. There are 15 unit squares.

TIME

The ongoing sequence of events. Time is the past, the present and the future. We measure time in seconds, minutes, hours, days, weeks, months, years, decades and centuries.

TIMES

Another word for multiply. Multiplication tells us how many times we have a number, so 'times' has become an accepted word to indicate this.

Example: 7 multiplied by 3 is written: 3 × 7 and often people will say 3 times 7, meaning that we have more than one 7, we have it 3 times. The symbol '×' is often called the times sign.

TON

A unit of weight equal to 2,000 pounds or 907.18 kilograms.

TRANSFORMATION

Moving a figure by a translation, reflection, or rotation. In a transformation a shape is moved to a different position, but it still has the same size, area, angles and lines.

Examples of transformations:

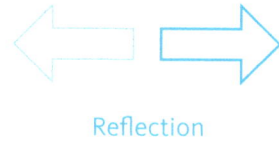

Translation

Rotation

Reflection

(See REFLECTION, ROTATION, TRANSLATION)

TRANSLATION

Moving or sliding an object a fixed distance in a given direction. In a translation, the resulting figure is congruent with the initial figure. Another name for a translation is a slide.

(See SLIDE, TRANSFORMATION)

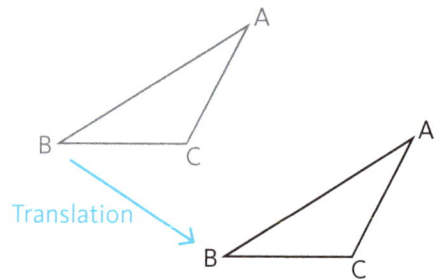

Translation

TRANSVERSAL

A straight line that intersects two or more different lines.

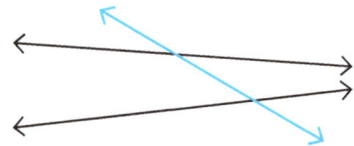

TRAPEZOID

A quadrilateral that has only one set of parallel sides. The parallel sides of a trapezoid are called the bases of the trapezoid. The other two sides are called the legs. In the UK the shape is called a trapezium.

Note: Some define a trapezoid as having at least one pair of parallel sides, which would mean that any parallelogram (a shape with two pair of parallel sides) would be classified as a trapezoid, but this is not the common definition.

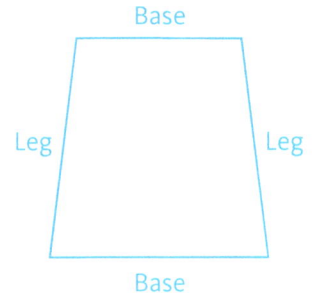

TREE DIAGRAM

A chart with a branching structure used to organize all possible outcomes of a process and often used to determine the probability of each.

Example: This tree diagram can determine the number of outcomes that are possible and may also be used to indicate the probability of each individual outcome occurring.

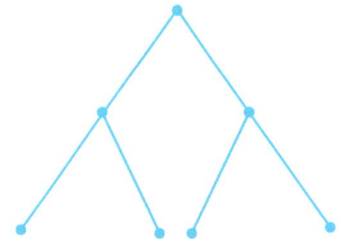

TREND

A general pattern found in a set of data.

TREND LINE

A line drawn on a scatter plot to closely fit the data points on the plot. A trend line on a graph shows the general direction of a group of points of data.

If one set of data increases when another set of related data also increases then the trend shown is called a positive trend. If one set of data decreases when the other set of related data increases then the trend shown is called a negative trend.

Note: Trend line is also known as line of best fit. Positive trend, negative trend and no trend are often referred to as positive correlation, negative correlation, and no correlation.

Example: The weight registered on a scale increases as you add pennies. The weight registered and the number of pennies would create a positive trend.

The money in your wallet decreases as you buy gifts. The more gifts you buy, the less money you have. This would graph as a negative trend line.

(See SCATTER PLOT)

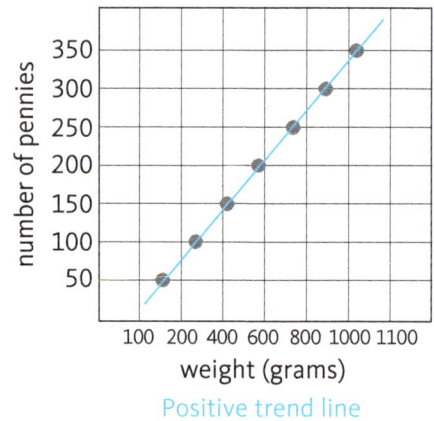

Positive trend line

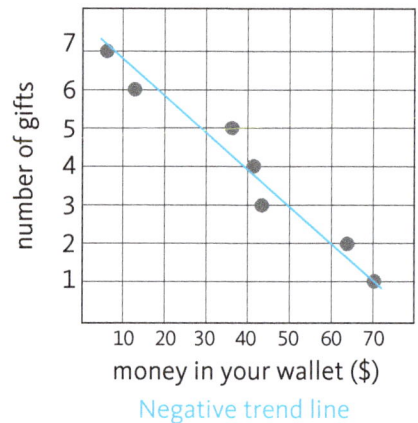

Negative trend line

TRIANGLE

A polygon with 3 sides and 3 angles.

Note: Triangles are commonly named by the three letters of their vertices.

(See POLYGON)

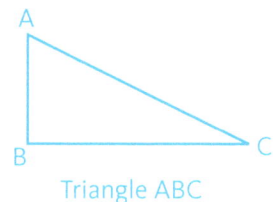

Triangle ABC

TRIANGULAR NUMBER

A number that can be represented by a triangular arrangement of equally spaced dots.

(See FIGURATE NUMBERS)

TRIGONOMETRY

The branch of mathematics that studies the relationships between the three sides and the three angles of a triangle. Each trigonometric function is a ratio of two sides of a right triangle.

(See COSINE, SECANT, SINE, TANGENT)

TRILLION

A number in base ten that is equal to 1 followed by 12 zeros or 10^{12} or 1,000,000,000,000.

TRINOMIAL

A polynomial with three terms.

Example: $3x^2 + 2x + 5$

TRIPLE

To make something three times as large. To triple a quantity you would multiply by 3.

Example: A triple dip ice cream cone has 3 dips of ice cream.

TRISECT

To cut something into 3 equal parts.

TRUNCATE

To cut something off. To drop digits following a decimal point without rounding.

Examples: A decimal string can be truncated after a given number of positions. 3.33333333333.... for ease of computation might be truncated after four positions to the right of the decimal point: 3.3333

A three-dimensional shape can be altered by cutting it, such as by removing the apex of a cone, or prism with a plane.

Truncated cone

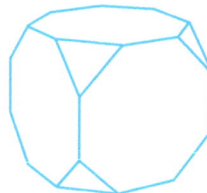
A truncated cube is created by truncating the tips of a cube

TURN

To rotate about a point. Note that in a turn, the distance from the point at the center of the rotation to any point on the shape stays the same. One complete turn is a full rotation of 360°.

(See ROTATE)

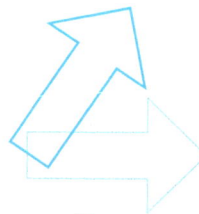
Turn

TWO DIMENSIONAL

A shape that only has two dimensions, width and height, but no depth. Two dimensional figures lie in a plane.

Examples: Polygons are two dimensional. Circles are two dimensional, but spheres are three dimensional.

(See DIMENSION)

U

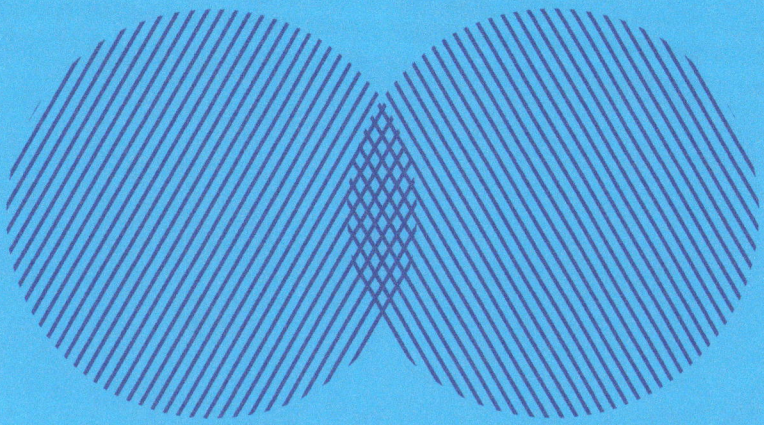
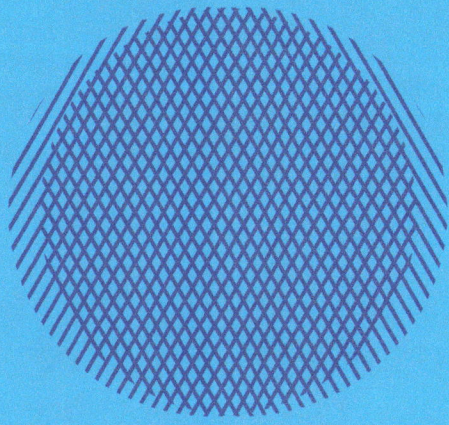
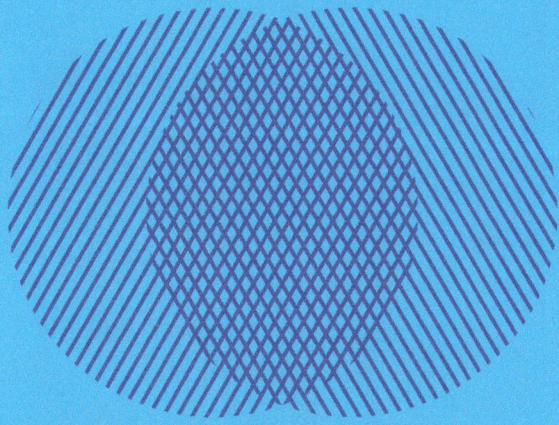
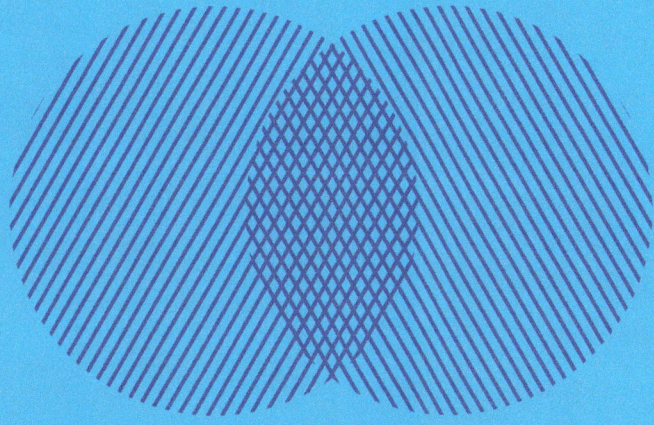
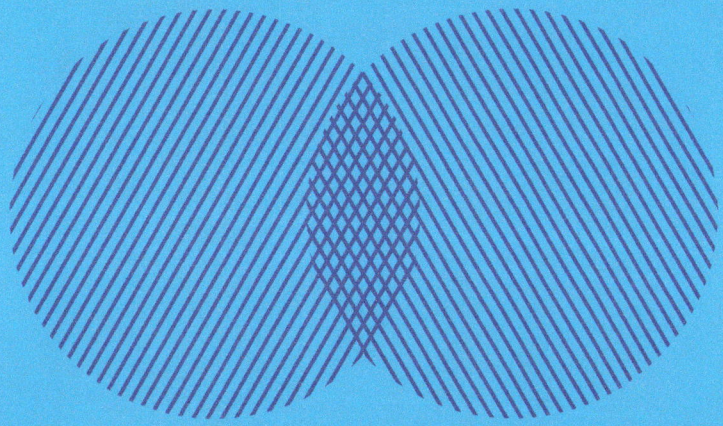

UNBIASED SAMPLE

A sample of data in which every member of the group being sampled had an equal chance of being included in the sample.

(See SAMPLE)

UNEQUAL

Not equal. The symbol for unequal is ≠.

Example: $5 \neq 6$

UNIFORM MOTION

Moving in a straight line at constant speed.

UNION OF SETS

The union of two sets, A and B, is the set of all elements in set A or set B or in both.

Examples: Set A consists of the elements A, B, C; set B consists of the elements C, D, E, F. The union of Set A with Set B is: A U B is the set A, B, C, D, E, F. Note that C is a member of both sets and a member of the union.

Some children in class have a dog and some have a cat and some have both. The union of the sets of children is those with a dog, a cat or both.

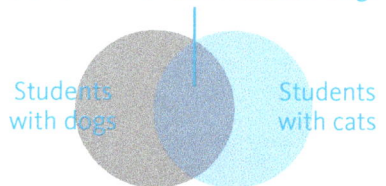

Students with both cats and dogs

Students with dogs

Students with cats

All the students are included in the union of the set

UNIT

A single thing. One.

UNIT CUBE

A unit of measure that is used to determine volume.
A unit cube has length, width, and depth of 1 unit.
The volume of a unit cube is 1 cubic unit.

1 unit cube

Example: The space inside this rectangular prism
is occupied by 18 unit cubes, so the volume of the
rectangular prism is 18 cubic units.

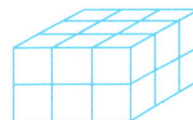

(3 x 2 x 3 unit cubes) =
18 cubic units

UNIT FRACTION

A proper fraction with a numerator of 1. If any whole is divided into B equal parts, then the amount formed by $\frac{1}{B}$ (or one of those parts) is the unit fraction.

Examples: $\frac{1}{3}$ is the unit fraction of a whole that has been divided into 3 equal parts.

$\frac{1}{10}$ is the unit fraction of a whole that has been divided into 10 equal parts.

UNIT OF MEASURE

A reference value used to measure. A unit of measure is the accepted one unit standard used in a measuring system.

Note: Different units are used to measure the same quantity in different measurement systems.

Examples: Mile and kilometer are standard units used to measure distance.
Gallon and liter are units used to measure capacity.
Kilogram and pound are used as units to measure the weight.

UNIT RATE

A rate that compares one quantity to one unit of another measure. A unit rate describes how many units of a first type of measurement correspond to one unit of the second type of measurement.

Example: A unit price is one type of unit rate. If the cost of a dozen eggs is $3.60, then the unit price is the unit rate of $0.30/egg.

(See RATE)

UNIT SQUARE

A unit of measure that is used to determine area. A unit square has length and width of 1 unit. The area of a unit square is 1 square unit.

Example: The space inside of the rectangle below is covered by 24 unit squares, so the area of the rectangle is 24 square units.

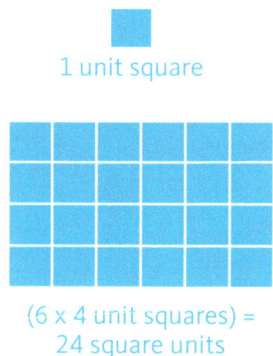

1 unit square

(6 x 4 unit squares) = 24 square units

(See TILING)

UNIVERSAL SET

The set that contains all possible elements under consideration.

Example: You may want to group the children in your class into several different sets, such as the set of children who have pets, the set of children who play soccer, the set of children who have apples in their lunch. The universal set for all these groupings is all the children in your class.

UNKNOWN

In an equation, the variable to be solved for. The solution of an equation is the value of the unknown.

Example: $X + 4 = 7$ X is the unknown and the solution of the equation is $X = 3$.

UNLIKE FRACTIONS

Fractions with different denominators.

Example: $\frac{1}{3}$ and $\frac{1}{5}$ are unlike fractions.

UPPER BOUND

The member of a set of numbers with a value equal to or greater than every other member of the set.

Example: The upper bound of the set {5, 5, 7, 9, 9, 11} is 11.

VALUE

The numerical worth of something. A fixed number that is applied to a variable is called the value. The result of a calculation is sometimes also called the value.

Examples: A penny has a value of 1¢.
In the equation $X + 4 = 9$, X has a value of 5.
$8 ÷ 4$ has a value of 2.

VANISHING POINT

The point at which parallel lines appear to meet as they recede into the distance. Parallel lines only appear to converge but, in fact, never do.

(See PARALLEL LINES)

VARIABLE

A letter or symbol that represents a quantity that is unknown and that may vary. Variables are used in algebra to indicate that the quantity is unknown. Variables are also used in formulas.

Examples: $x + 5 = 8$. x is unknown until the equation is solved.

The formula for the area of a rectangle can be given as $A = l × w$. The area, represented by A, will vary with the values of the length (l) and width (w).

Note: If we can make an equation out of an ordinary statement by using variables, it will make solving a problem much easier.

Example: Mary had 8 apples. John gave her more apples, and then she had 11. How many apples did John give to Mary? If we let the variable X equal the number of apples John gave to Mary, then we can write the problem in an equation: $8 + X = 11$

(See ALGEBRA)

VARIANCE

Indicates the spread in a set of data. In statistics, the variance tells us how measured data in a set of data vary from the average value of the set.

VECTOR

A quantity that has both magnitude and direction. Vectors represent magnitude and direction at the same time as a ray that has length and a direction (the way it points.) Vectors are often used in physics and navigation.

Example: Wind has both a speed and a direction and can be expressed as a vector.

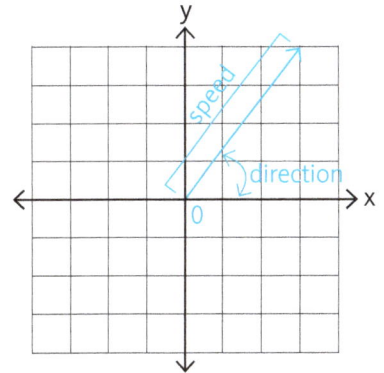

VELOCITY

The rate of change of the position of an object over a given time. Velocity tells how fast something is changing position (its speed) and in which direction. Both speed and direction are required to define velocity.

(See ACCELERATION, SPEED, VECTOR)

VENN DIAGRAM

A diagram that uses closed curves (usually circles) to graph the relationships among sets. The members of each set are represented within the area inside the circle. A Venn diagram will give a clear picture of where the sets intersect (members of both sets appear in an overlapping area) or if they are disjoint (with no members that belong to both). It is named after John Venn, a British logician and philosopher, who first used this type of diagram.

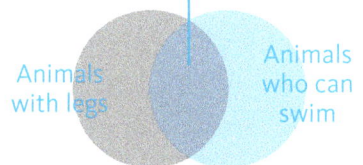

Venn diagram for two sets with **some** shared, or common, attributes

Disjoint set: Venn diagram for two sets with **no** shared, or common, attributes

VERTEX

1) The point where two or more straight lines or line segments meet.

A is the vertex

2) The intersection point of two sides of a plane figure.

Example: The angles of a polygon are its vertices.

ABC and D are vertices

3) A point shared by three or more sides of a solid figure.

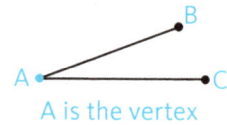

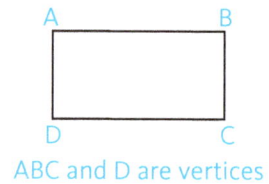

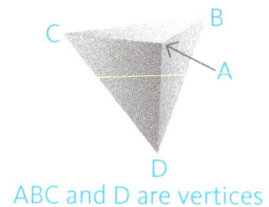

ABC and D are vertices

VERTICAL

In an up-down position. Upright. A straight up and down line is called a vertical line.

VERTICAL ANGLES

The angles opposite each other when two lines intersect. Also called opposite angles.

Example: A and B, the pair of angles opposite each other formed by two intersecting lines, are vertical angles.

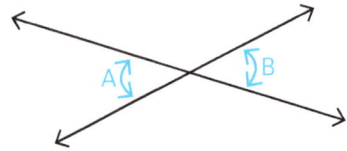

VERTICAL AXIS

(See AXIS definition 2, Y AXIS)

VERTICAL BAR GRAPH

A graph that displays data using vertical bars. The lengths of the bars on a bar graph are proportional to the quantities they represent.

Note: Bar graphs are used when one set of data on the graph doesn't have a numerical scale.

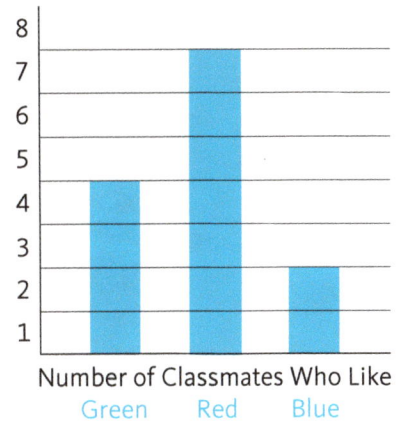

Number of Classmates Who Like
Green   Red   Blue

VOLUME

The amount of 3 dimensional space an object occupies. Volume is the amount of space inside of something like a cube or a cylinder. The volume of a container tells us how much the container can hold.

Note: Volume is always measured using linear measurements such as inches or centimeters and the dimensions are expressed as cubed, meaning in three dimensions.

The formula for the volume of this box is V = length × width × height.

Example: If the length is 10 inches, the width is 4 inches and the height is 6 inches, the volume is:
v = 10 × 4 × 6 or 240 cubic inches.

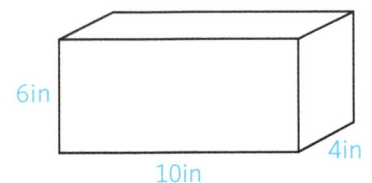

6in

10in   4in

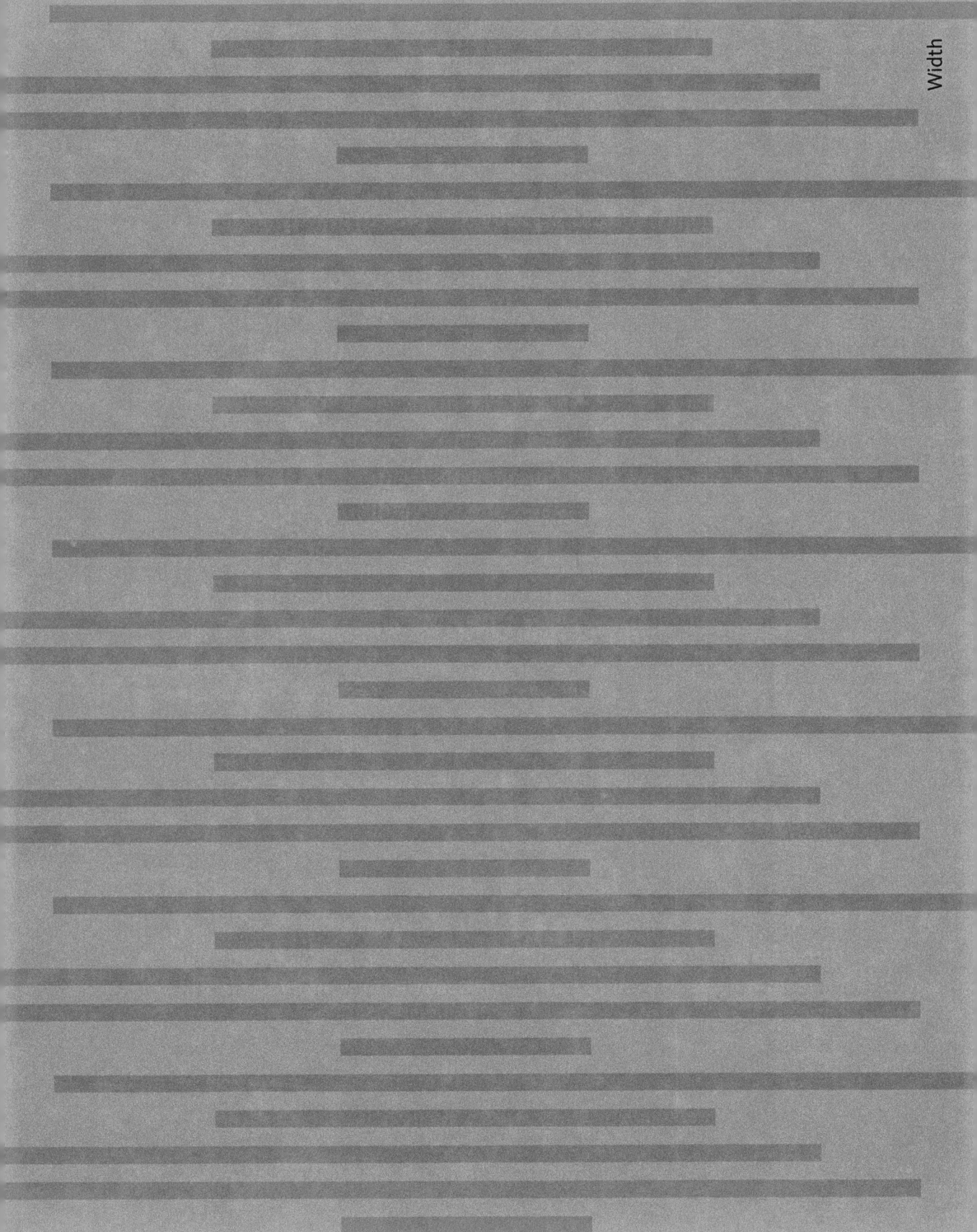

WEIGHT

The downward force gravity has on an object. Weight tells us how heavy something is. We often confuse mass of with weight, but because the force of gravity changes, weight can change with location. Mass remains the same.

To calculate weight you can multiply mass by the force of gravity at that point.

Example: Gravity on earth at sea level is equal to 1, or 1 g. Gravity on the moon is approximately $\frac{1}{6}$ of that on earth, or $\frac{1}{6}$ g. You would weigh only $\frac{1}{6}$ as much on the moon.

The abbreviation for gravity is the same as the abbreviation we use for gram (g); be careful not to confuse the two.

Note: Though weight and mass are different, weight often uses the same standard measurement units of mass such as grams and kilograms or ounces and pounds.

WHOLE NUMBERS

The set of all counting numbers plus zero. Whole numbers are 0, 1, 2, 3, 4, 5, 6, 7, 8, 9, 10, 11... These numbers do not have a fractional or decimal part, and negative numbers are not part of the set of whole numbers. The set of whole numbers is infinite.

Note: The counting numbers are also called natural numbers.

(See COUNTING NUMBERS, NATURAL NUMBERS)

WIDTH

The measure of distance from side to side of a two or three dimensional figure. Width is a linear measure, meaning that it is measured in units of length.

(See MEASUREMENT)

WRITTEN FORM

A number written as it is spoken. Sometimes called word form.

Examples: The written form of 13 is thirteen; the written form of $\frac{1}{5}$ is one fifth.

X

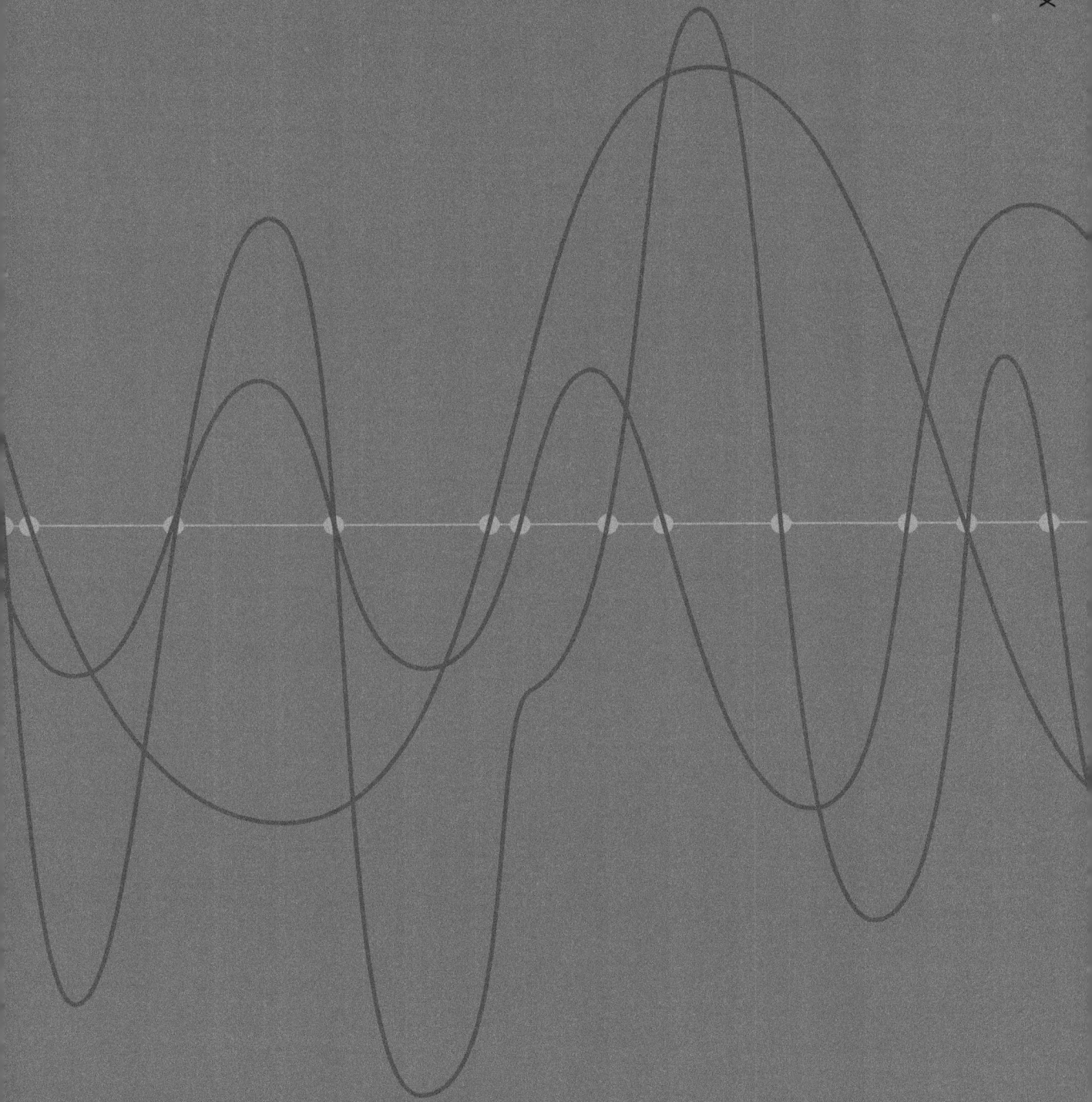

X

Often used in algebra to mean a value that is not yet known.

(See VARIABLE)

X AXIS

Commonly the horizontal axis in a Cartesian coordinate system. The Cartesian coordinate system, or the coordinate plane, is formed by the intersection of two number lines, a horizontal number line and a vertical number line. The horizontal number line is commonly called the x axis.

(See AXIS, CARTESIAN COORDINATE SYSTEM)

X COORDINATE

The location of a point along the x axis. Commonly the first number in an ordered pair, the X coordinate locates a point along the x axis in a Cartesian coordinate system.

(See CARTESIAN COORDINATE SYSTEM, ORDERED PAIR. X AXIS)

X INTERCEPT

If a line or a curve graphed on a Cartesian coordinate system crosses the x axis, the value of X at the point it crosses the x axis.

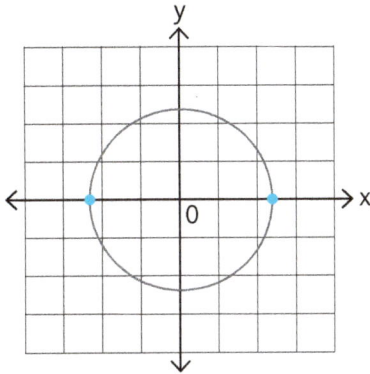

A circle can have two x intercepts

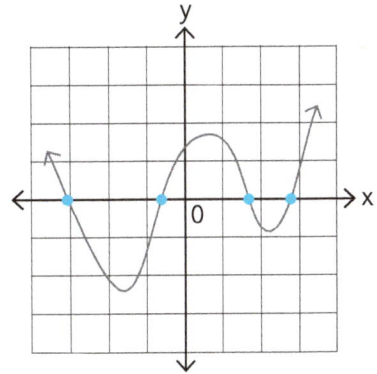

A curve can have many x intercepts

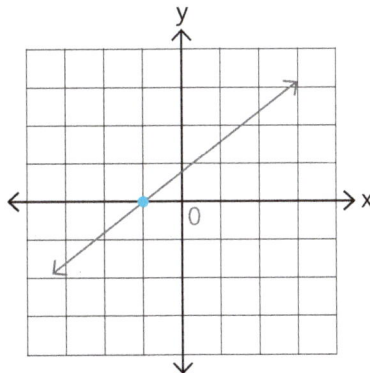

A straight line that is not on the x axis and is not parellel to the x axis will have one x intercept

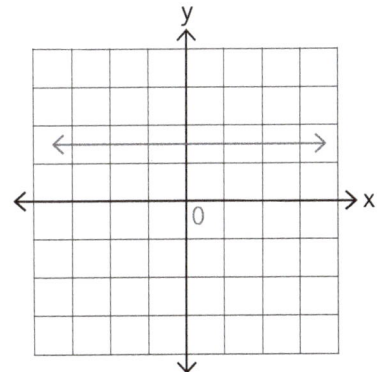

A straight line that is parellel to the x axis, but not on the x axis, will have no x intercept

(See CARTESIAN COORDINATE SYSTEM, X AXIS)

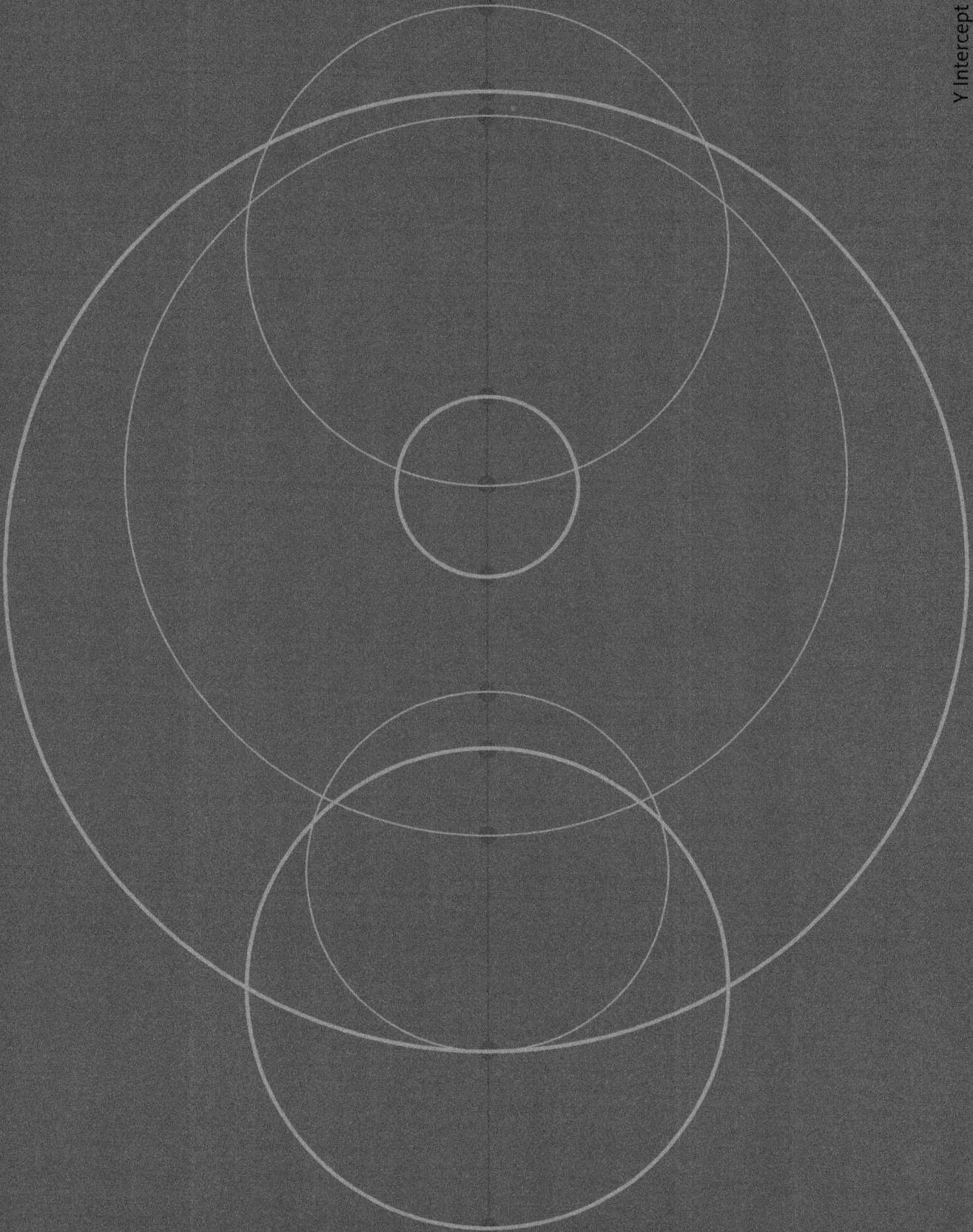

Y AXIS

Commonly the vertical axis in a Cartesian coordinate system. The Cartesian coordinate system, or the coordinate plane, is formed by the intersection of two number lines, a horizontal number line and a vertical number line. The vertical number line is commonly called the y axis.

(See AXIS, CARTESIAN COORDINATE SYSTEM)

Y COORDINATE

The location of a point along the y axis. Commonly the second number in an ordered pair, the Y coordinate locates a point along the y axis in a Cartesian coordinate system.

(See CARTESIAN COORDINATE SYSTEM, ORDERED PAIR)

Y INTERCEPT

If a line or a curve graphed on a Cartesian coordinate system crosses the y axis, the value of Y at the point it crosses the y axis.

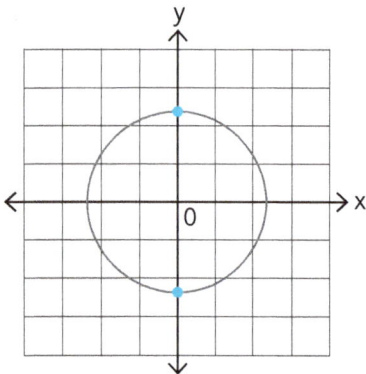

A circle can have two y intercepts

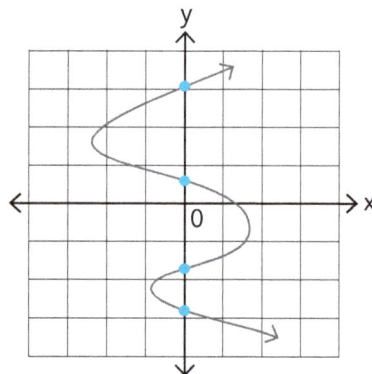

A curve can have many y intercepts

continued ⟶

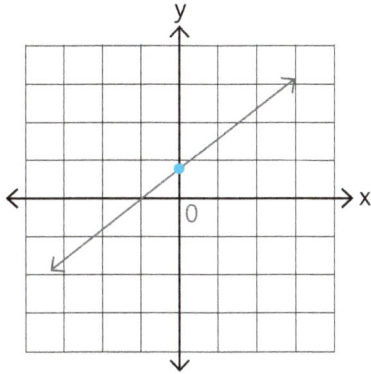

A straight line that is not on the y axis and is not parellel to the y axis will have one y intercept

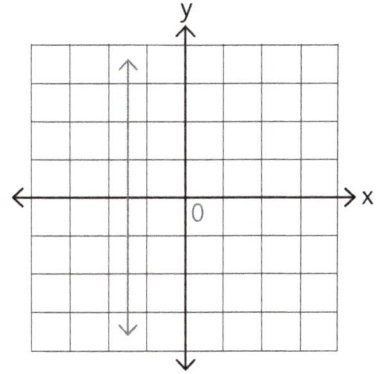

A straight line that is parellel to the y axis, but not on the y axis, will have no y intercept

(See CARTESIAN COORDINATE SYSTEM, Y AXIS)

YARD

A unit of length in the customary measurement system. Abbreviated yds.

1 yard = 3 feet
1 yard = 36 inches

(See MEASUREMENT)

YEAR

The period of time in which the Earth makes a complete revolution around the sun. We measure a year in 365 days, from January 1 to December 31, but this measurement is approximate and we must adjust our calendar once every four years by adding an extra day to the month of February.

ZERO

The whole number between -1 and 1. The symbol we use for zero is 0.

0 is a digit in every place value numbering system and indicates that there is no value in the space it occupies. 0 is the identity element for addition because, when 0 is added to a second number, the sum is always equal to the second number itself.

Note: The plural of zero is either zeros or zeroes; both are correct.

(See IDENTITY ELEMENT, PLACE VALUE)

ZERO DIMENSIONAL

Having no dimension, neither length nor height nor depth. A point has no dimension, it is just a location. It occupies no space. We usually represent a point by a dot, but a dot has some dimension; a point does not.

ZERO PRODUCT PROPERTY

The product of any real number and 0 is 0. (Also called the zero property of multiplication.) When the product of two or more factors is equal to 0, then at least one of the factors must be zero.

Examples of $n \times 0 = 0$ for every real number n:
$3 \times 0 = 0$ and $0 \times 3 = 0$
$96589 \times 0 = 0$
$\frac{1}{6} \times 0 = 0$
$\pi \times 0 = 0$

CONTRIBUTORS

M.W. Penn

With a degree in mathematics, Ms. Penn began her career designing software for AT&T, the University of Florida and the FDA. Eager to encourage young students to embrace math, she began writing children's books focused on mathematics concepts and is an award winning author of 19 books; titles include *Square Bear: a fairytale of polygons, Empress Adelaide Dances at 8: a time telling tale* and a Young Adult novel, *The Pèlerin of the Orb,* which won the Communication Award from both the Connecticut Press Club and the National Federation of Press Women. She has co-authored a teachers' guide to lesson plans which introduce elementary math concepts through stories: *Children's Literature in the K-3 Mathematics Classroom: 50 activities based on the CCSS.* Her poetry appears in Highlights for Children and in several anthologies.

Ms. Penn presents sessions at state, regional and national conferences of the National Council of Teachers of Mathematics and has chaired a session on interdisciplinary learning at the annual conference of the National Council of Teachers of English.

Monica Merritt, Ed.D.

Monica Merritt, Ed.D. has been involved in mathematics education for over twenty years, teaching mathematics in public and private K-12 schools in both New York and Connecticut and serving as mathematics department chair. Currently an Associate Professor of Education at Mount Saint Mary College in Newburgh, New York, Dr. Merritt teaches elementary and secondary mathematics methods and content area literacy courses to pre-service and in-service teachers. She is interested in problem solving in the K-8 curriculum and the use of graphic organizers in mathematics.

She lives in New York with her husband, Brian, and daughters Jasmine and Morgan.

Daphne Firos

Daphne Firos is an award winning designer with broad experience across all forms of graphic design, including environmental branding, identity, editorial design and illustration. She has worked as a designer and strategist throughout the US and Europe, and she has also taught in the School of Visual Communication Design at Kent State University.

You can see more of her work at *www.studiofiros.com.*

MathWord Press
www.mathwordpress.com

www.mathwordpress.com

ADDITIONAL MATHWORD PRESS TITLES

2 Lines, a story of straight lines and curves

A Tangram ABC, shaping the alphabet from an ancient Chinese puzzle

Children's Literature In The K-3 Mathematics Classroom, 50 Activities Based on the Common Core State Standards for Mathematics

Empress Adelaide Dances at 8, a time telling tale

Flibberty Digits and Flummery Daubs, magical, madcap math, a book of poetry

Sidney the Silly Who Only Eats 6, a fairytale comparing numbers

Square Bear and *Square Bear Meets Round Hound*, fairytales in polygons and curves

That's Not a Beagle, a study of attributes

The Pèlerin of the Orb, a young adult novel of Malice, Mysticism and Mathematics

www.ingramcontent.com/pod-product-compliance
Lightning Source LLC
Chambersburg PA
CBHW061228150426
42812CB00054BA/2546

* 9 7 8 1 9 3 9 4 3 1 0 7 3 *